FREEMASONRY

F O R   B E G I N N E R S ®

FREEMASONRY
FOR BEGINNERS®

BY ROBERT LOMAS • ILLUSTRATIONS BY SARAH BECAN

Foreword by Gordon Echlin

FOR BEGINNERS®

For Beginners LLC
30 Main Street, Suite 303
Danbury, CT 06810 USA
www.forbeginnersbooks.com

A For Beginners® Documentary Comic Book

Copyright © 2017

Cataloging-in-Publication information is
available from the Library of Congress.

ISBN-13: 978-1-939994-56-1

Manufactured in the United States of America

For Beginners® and Beginners Documentary Comic
Books® are published by For Beginners LLC.
First Edition

10 9 8 7 6 5 4 3 2 1

Contents

FOREWORD

by Gordon Echlin

Y ou are holding a very dangerous book in your hands! How is that, you ask?

As a non-Mason, you are reading a brief but comprehensive overview of a mysterious organization whose most superficial aspects have not historically been open to inspection. It is an organization with a reputation for power and ruthlessness. No doubt you will learn some insidious and frightening secrets that might put you on a list of persons marked for "innocuous accident." Better not let anybody see you reading this book! And remember, the "walls have eyes"!

Or ... on the other hand ... you may be disappointed to learn the truth of the matter: that the ideals and intent of Freemasonry are ennobling and altruistic, that it is neither a sinister religion nor an organization plotting a New World Order. *Really?*

If perhaps you are already a Freemason, this book may turn aspects of your world upside down. You are being introduced to a well-researched, definitive history of "the Craft." This history is different from the constructed party line—the one that says four lodges met in London in 1717 and magically precipitated the fraternity out of thin air. It also rains on the glorious legendary chivalric links to the Knights Templar. *Say it isn't so!*

But keep reading. You may find the real history of Freemasonry more fulfilling than the one you knew. The mundane view of your own "hobby" may be turned on its head to reveal a pathway to enlightenment that you have been obstinately ignoring, despite the constant exhortations to higher ideals. *What? It's not all about dressing up, play acting, pompous rank, and a good night out with the boys? How bothersome!*

Dr. Robert Lomas—Brother Dr. Robert Lomas to fellow Freemasons—has been upending the world of Freemasonry since the mid-1990s , beginning with his book *The Hiram Key* (co-authored with Christopher Knight). Both Masons and the rest of the world have been all the better for it. My own introduction to his writing was probably similar to the kind of clandestine first experience of many Masons-to-be. It began with a book containing information I thought I shouldn't have and morphed into a recognition this ancient society is a tonic for the malaise of superficiality, materialism, and social isolation that grips today's world of the Internet, social media, and video gaming.

From that point on, the true nature of Freemasonry began to reveal itself to me. And it was on my very doorstep—indeed everybody's doorstep in the Western Hemisphere, with a Lodge in almost every small community and multiple Lodges in large metropolitan areas. After some consideration, I eagerly joined with a friend. Neither of us has waned in enthusiasm ever since. That is not necessarily a given, as there are shoals in Freemasonry on which one can easily become stranded. Throughout, I have always had a secret weapon in my pocket: the books of Robert Lomas.

And so, from those early days, Dr. Lomas's books have helped me understand and appreciate Freemasonry—a tradition and set of beliefs that don't reveal their true nature easily. He is a renaissance man of sorts, a lettered physicist with an abiding interest in archaeology, history, and symbology. He is even rumored to be the archetype for Dan Brown's globetrotting symbolist sleuth, Dr. Robert Langdon (without the pyrotechnics), in The Da Vinci Code (2003) and succeeding novels. But Dr. Lomas's academic background and scientific perspective are what have most struck a chord with me, allowing me to reconcile ancient philosophic mystery teachings with a modern worldview defined by quantum physics. There is a certain poetry in this, as the two worlds are now converging more than diverging. If you don't know that, well, here is another reason to read Dr. Lomas's books.

In recent years, Dr. Lomas and I have been introduced via the fraternal bonds we share and a similar view of "the Craft," as we call it. It is truly a global network that allows members from far-flung lands to connect on the same level, with a shared understanding, no matter their social status.

So I hope I have piqued your interest in this topic and this book! Freemasonry is rich and deep, and Dr. Robert Lomas—Brother Robert Lomas—is just the person to introduce its many facets in a way that MUST matter to the inquiring mind in the 21st century.

One last caution. Perhaps the greatest danger of *Freemasonry For Beginners* is that you read it, think you understand it all, and move on. You will never really understand Freemasonry until you experience it firsthand and engage with it fully. If you don't join, don't think you understand it, even if you read every book written on the subject. Freemasonry is an experiential science.

Gordon Echlin is a Past Master of St. John's Lodge, No. 63 on the Grand Registry of Canada; Past First Principal, Maple-Granite Chapter No. 61; and a Grand Officer in the Grand Chapter of Royal Arch Masons of Canada in the Province of Ontario.

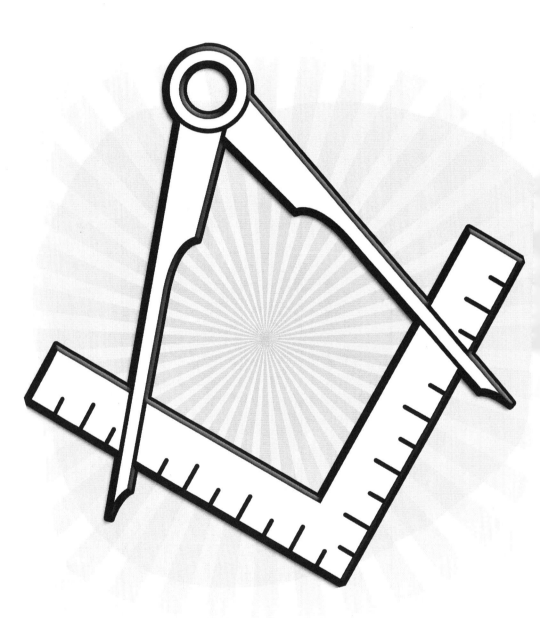

INTRODUCTION

MANY PEOPLE HAVE HEARD OF FREEMASONRY, but few have any idea what it is, what it does, or why it exists. This book will tell you all the basic facts about what Freemasonry is, what it does, and why it remains active today.

Freemasonry is older than the United States. It played an important role in the pursuit of independence and in the writing of the American Constitution. The Craft of Masonry teaches a peculiar symbology and carries out secret rituals in closed and guarded rooms that only members may enter.

It is thought to be a male-dominated organization, but there are branches that allow only women to be members. A Woman Freemason is still called a Brother, which does seem odd at first. There are other branches (called Co-Masonry) that allow both men and women to join the same group.

A group of Freemasons is called a **lodge**. Each lodge has a name and a number and meets at regular times. The lodge number is given by a central organization of the branch of Freemasonry in the area where the lodge was formed. This central group, which keeps a roll of all the lodges created in its name, is called a Grand Lodge. Regular lodge meetings may be held on a weekly, monthly, or quarterly basis. In them, members perform teaching rituals and meet socially. After the meeting, they often they share a meal called the Festive Board.

Most countries in the world have a Grand Lodge, and some have more than one. For example, the United Kingdom has three male Grand Lodges—for Scotland, Ireland, and England (including Wales)—and a female Grand Lodge for the entire UK. In the United States, every state has at least one male Grand Lodge and some have more than one. Before the emancipation of slaves, a separate system of male lodges was set up for black brethren, called Prince Hall Lodges. Today there also separate Grand Lodges for women only and for mixed membership. All Grand Lodges, as well as the lodges they have warranted and numbered, share a common philosophy. They study and teach a common system of symbolism, and they promote an ethos that encourages charity and good works.

Freemasonry began as a self-help society, assisting members to learn about themselves and to improve their moral fiber. It has also maintained a longstanding commitment to civic responsibility and charitable work. Members have included presidents, jazz musicians, astronauts, soldiers, cowboys, scientists, aviators, film makers, actors, magicians, and others.

Here are a few Americans you might recognize: George Washington, Paul Revere, John Hancock, John Paul Jones, Duke Ellington, Nat King Cole, Lionel Hampton, Dizzy Gillespie, Paul Robeson, Buzz Aldrin, John Glenn, Gus Grissom, Douglas Macarthur, John Pershing, Kit Carson, Jim Bowie, Roy Rogers, Benjamin Franklin, Samuel Colt, Charles Lindbergh, Eddie Rickenbacker, Louis B. Mayer, John Wayne, Audie Murphy, and Harry Houdini.

As you can see from this list, Freemasonry has attracted many creative and successful people from all segments of society and all walks of life. Add in Wolfgang Mozart, Enrico Fermi, and Franklin D. Roosevelt, and you can see the kind of diverse backgrounds and achievements that have typified the membership in diverse times and locations.

WHAT IS IT about Freemasonry that has inspired so many leaders and shakers to become part of this odd-ball order? To answer that we need first to look at how the organization began and think about what it teaches that so inspires members.

Freemasonry is a spiritual self-help society whose declared purpose is to help members become better citizens, and it has a strong track record in doing this. It began in Scotland during the 15th century.

The first lodge of Freemasons for which we have records is the Lodge of Aberdeen. We know that the lodge was employed to build St. Nicholas's Kirk in the city of Aberdeen during the second half of the 15th century and that the lodge created a floorcloth covered in ancient symbols, used to teach apprentices. We also know the names of two of the earliest masters of the lodge: David Menzies and Matthew Wright, both stonemasons.

Menzies and Wright had been made redundant after working on Rosslyn Chapel, the strange building in southeastern Scotland that was the focus of Dan Brown's bestselling novel *The Da Vinci Code* (2003). When these two men founded the Lodge of Aberdeen in the 1480s, they began the systematic study of symbols that became a key feature of Freemasonry's long-term success. They recorded the main symbols of Freemasonry and began to develop the ritual teaching methods that have inspired so many people ever since.

At around the same time, the lodge created a floorcloth that shows all the symbols still used in Freemasonry today. Carbon dating of the original floorcloth confirms the period when the lodge first began to study symbolism.

The Lodge of Aberdeen founded a system of teaching based on the study of symbols, the art of memory, and an urge to discover a purpose in life. The members did this by studying the hidden mysteries of nature and science to better understand the work and aims of the Great Architect of the Universe.

Freemasonry is not, and never has been, a religion. It is a philosophy that brings together people who think there is a purpose to life and allows them to discuss what they have in common. It forbids the discussion of topics that might cause argument, such as religion and politics. Freemasonry defines itself as *"a peculiar system of morality, veiled in allegory and illustrated by symbols."* By "peculiar" it does not mean odd, but singular or unique. It teaches morality and encourages the practice of three great principles:

Love for your fellow humans;

Charity towards the less fortunate; and

Search for the Truth about the nature of yourself and the world you live in.

A POWERFUL PHILOSOPHY of self-help and self-improvement, Freemasonry has spread across the globe. Today there are approximately 3 million active Freemasons belonging to over 46,000 lodges in every country in the world. About 70% of the world's Freemasons live in the Americas—57% in the United States, 10% in South and Central America, and 3% in Canada. About 24% of the world's Freemasons live in Europe, with the remaining 6% spread roughly equally across Asia, Africa, and Australia.

The number and size of lodges also differ from continent to continent. About 50% of the world's Masonic lodges are located in the Americas, with about 29% in the United States. U.S. lodges tend to have more members than those in the rest of the world, with an average of more than 100. In South America, there are about 36 Masons in each lodge, while the average in Canada is 68. Europe, where Freemasonry began, is home to 42% of the world's Masonic lodges, but the average lodge membership is only 33. Worldwide, the average lodge membership is 58.

Asia, Australia, and the Americas tend to have fewer lodges with more members per lodge, while Europe and Africa have more lodges but fewer members. This pattern is related to the length of time over which lodges have been established in particular countries. In Scotland, where Freemasonry began, the average lodge membership is 30. In England and Wales, two of the first countries to which it spread, the average lodge membership is 29. And in Ireland, which also adopted Freemasonry in its early stages, the average lodge membership today is 20.

Every Freemasonic Lodge must fill a specific set of positions in order to carry out its ritual teachings and to conduct administrative business. The members who fill the ritual positions are called Officers of the Lodge, and there are eight of them: two guards, two deacons, two wardens, a worshipful master, and an immediate past master. The seven administrative roles to be filled are: secretary, director of ceremonies, treasurer, almoner, chaplain, organist, and steward. Thus, a minimum of 15 members are needed to run a lodge.

To become the Worshipful Master of a lodge, a new member must first complete three degrees: Entered Apprentice, Fellowcraft, and Master Mason. Then the member must serve a year in each offices of the lodge, in strict order. (Each office teaches a different set of skills to the Mason who holds it.) Thus, it takes about ten years to reach the office of Worshipful Master in a lodge of 20 members.

If a lodge has more members, it is likely to take longer to reach the rank of Worshipful Master, as other members will be awaiting the chance to serve in each office. When a lodge gets too big and the waiting time gets too long, it creates a new daughter lodge. This ensures that more members can progress through the offices and learn the lessons of each rank. The optimum size of a lodge to ensure continuity and easy progression to Worshipful Master is about 30.

The pattern can be seen in the relative number of lodges and members in the continents where Freemasonry has been established the longest. For example, Europe has 24% of the world's Masons but 42% of the world's lodges, whereas the Americas have 72% of the world's Masons but only 50% of the world's lodges.

Europe has an average lodge membership of 33, which is close to optimal, while the higher average in the Americas—80—suggests that these areas face considerable pressure to create new daughter lodges, speed up progression, and facilitate teaching methods.

THE MASONIC METHOD of teaching has many useful benefits. It teaches members how to memorize facts and information; it teaches them to understand the meanings of symbols; it teaches them to care about others; and it teaches them how to speak in public. Above all, it teaches members to seek a purpose for their lives and offers a way to achieve that purpose.

One of the basic principles of Freemasonry is that prospective members are not invited to join. If a person wants to become a Freemason, then he or she must ask about it. Anyone who does so will be welcomed at the local lodge, and the brethren will be happy to talk about the Craft.

Although the uninitiated often associate Freemasonry with secret signs, these are primarily the passwords, handshakes, and grips that enable members to identify themselves as among those who have qualified for each of the degrees. Everything else that Masons do, they are free to talk about. The real secrets of Freemasonry are the understandings and insights gained from carrying out the teaching rituals, which have been honed over hundreds of years. They have a powerful impact, helping members to expand and develop their thinking. These secrets cannot be stolen or given away, they can only be experienced.

THIS BOOK EXPLORES the objectives and teaching methods of Freemasonry and describes its influence on society in the past, present, and future. It recounts the origins of the movement in Scotland, its spread to North America and the rest of the world, and a mythical history that traces its descent from Adam down to Zerubbabel. Not least of all, it shows how Masonic teachings have helped so many members over the centuries learn the skills to become leaders in society, science, and the arts.

THE ORIGINS OF
FREEMASONRY

REEMASONRY HAS TWO SEPARATE HISTO-
RIES. It has a ritual history that begins in the Masonic Year
of Light, or *Anno Lucis* (A.L.). According to ritual myths, Freemasonry began with Adam, was passed down the lines of the patri-
archs to the builders of Solomon's Temple, and continued down to
the present day. The Masonic calen-
dar begins in the year 4000 B.C.E.,
said to be the year Adam was created, and is known as the year 1
A.L. The Masonic calendar is
4,000 years longer than the Christian calendar of Anno Domini
(A.D.) In other words, the year
2016 A.D. (or C.E.) is 6016 A.L. in
the Masonic Calendar.

FREEMASONRY ALSO HAS A MUNDANE HISTORY, WHICH IS LESS WELL-KNOWN AND NOT AS WIDELY TAUGHT.

ADAM

ABRAHAM

DAVID

SOLOMON

ZERUBBABEL

It begins with the names, date, and place where the masters of the first Freemasonic Lodge began to use the ritual history as a teaching aid to help them and their members develop an understanding of themselves and the world in which they lived. It proceeds to tell the story of how Freemasonry was spread and by whom.

The teaching method of Freemasonry is based on a simple idea. It is generally easier to grasp a concept if the facts are explained to you as a memorable story and then you then act out the

8

story to help learn its lessons. Thus, the teaching principle adopted by the first Freemasons is summarized in the adage,

Freemasonry involves members in its stories so they can understand the deep morals contained in them and appreciate the meaning of ancient symbols that predate written language.

The first Freemasons stumbled upon two powerful concepts. The first was that symbols can convey feelings and insights that are beyond the ability of language to capture but that may contain Truth. The second was that a story tells far more than a list of facts does. But what is the extra information that a story conveys?

When we tell a story about someone, we relate a series of episodes from their life that describes how they developed as a person in response to things that happened to them. What separates a story from a list of events is all the connections we instinctively feel between the sequence of events. If we believe there is a purpose to life, then we will search for connections between actions and their consequences.

A Peculiar System of Morality

Freemasonry describes itself in ritual as *"a peculiar system of morality, veiled in allegory, and illustrated by symbols."* It began when a small group of illiterate individuals recognized that there were two types of things in the world. There were things like stones or hammers that could be explained completely by listing their properties. For a stone, these included such attributes as its roughness, its smoothness, and its squareness or crookedness when used as a building block. For a

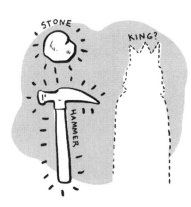

hammer, weight and balance helped a working Mason to visualize or describe it. But there were also things—such as kings, temples, and symbols—that could be explained only by telling their stories. For this second type of thing, a simple description was not enough. For example, you had to hear a story to explain why Solomon wanted to build a temple, why a temple would need two pillars at its entrance, and why the center of a perfect circle is a magical point.

By good fortune, we know the names two of the individuals who had this insight. They were David Menzies and Matthew Wright, members of a lodge of working stonemasons who, by their study of symbols and stories, first devised the processes of Freemasonry. Their actions were recorded in the minutes of the Burgh Council of Aberdeen, and their insights survive in a wonderful drawing of the symbols they used for teaching. Menzies and

Wright recognized that people, symbols, and cultures are not simply things, but are processes that unfold over time. Although they wouldn't have explained it that way, they certainly saw that there are only two types of things—objects and processes. Objects don't change, but processes do. Moreover, processes can change objects.

SOLOMON'S TEMPLE

If you want to change your-self and understand the world in which you live, then you must do more than simply learn facts. You must search for a way of changing and improving your-self. The analogy Menzies and Wright used was that of the most beautiful building in the ancient world, King Solomon's Temple. It was created by shaping many rough stones into highly polished parts of a graceful and beautiful structure.

Here's a little story about how they came to be in this position.

The First Recorded Lodge

The first written reference to a lodge of Masons appears in the records of the Aberdeen Burgh Council on June 27, 1483. According to the entry, the council decided that David Menzies, the master of church work, would be appointed master of the Masons of the Lodge. A later notation in the Aberdeen Burgh Council minutes, from 1493, says that Alexander Stuart, then the Master of the Lodge, was also elected to serve as an Alderman on the council. His Masonic training, it seemed, was helping make him a more effective member of society.

The lodge taught prospective members the methods of self-improvement used by the lodge, and they went on to become important members of Aberdeen society.

The Lodge of Aberdeen created drawings of the ancient symbols still employed in Masonic teaching today. The symbols were depicted

KIRKWALL SCROLL

on a decorated canvas carpet, known as a floorcloth. It was laid in the center of the lodge so the Masons could walk a ritual path of pilgrimage through the symbols. This was a powerful way of studying them. The original floorcloth moved to Orkney in 1786, when William Graham gifted it to Lodge Kirkwall Kilwinning. (Graham's merchant father had acquired it while trading in Aberdeen.) According to carbon dating, the central panel of the cloth dates to 1430–1530; the outer sections date to 1780–1840, the period in which it was given to the Kirkwall Lodge.

To answer that question, we have to go even farther back in time. In 1411, a powerful Scottish noble decided to build an alternative religious center to rival the Abbey of the Holyrood. The Abbey of the

Holyrood was said to house a fragment of the True Cross that had been brought to Scotland by Queen Margaret, the mother of King David I. The Holy Rood (Scots for Holy Cross) was owned by the Stuart kings of Scotland and was said to have protected David from a raging stag. This miracle, still symbolized in the entrance to ruins of the abbey, showed the common people that God favored the Stuart line of kings.

William St Clair, Lord Chancellor and High Admiral of Scotland, was the second-most powerful man in the kingdom. Between 1411 and 1446, he set out to build a shrine for his family that would match the power of Holyrood. Hoping it would inspire divine respect from the common people, he employed a man well-versed in the arts of symbolism, storytelling, architecture, and politics. That man was Sir Gilbert Hay, the author of three textbooks: *The Book of Armies*, which deals with the principles of warfare; *The Book of the Order of Knighthood*, a manual of knightly chivalry; and *The Book of the Governance of Princes*, which explains methods of gaining and using political power.

Hay assembled and supervised a large workforce of stonemasons to the south of Edinburgh in the village of Roslin, adjacent to the St Clair Castle. He set them to work carving a wonderfully ornate chapel, which survives to this day. The chapel was based on the layout of Solomon's Temple. Hay insisted that all its symbols were first carved into wood, and he inspected them before they were cut into stones for the building. In this way, the masons who worked for him saw the power of displaying symbols to tell stories in public buildings.

ROSSLYN CHAPEL

William St Clair's motive for building Rosslyn Chapel was to create a mausoleum collegiate church. He hoped it would provide a public focus for the St Clair family and promote him as a potential king for a partitioned Scotland. He intended to split the Stuart kingdom of Scotland into three parts—a third for himself; a third for John MacDonald, the Lord of Isles; and a third for Edward IV of England. The plot failed, and William's empire was broken up to ensure that the St Clair family could never again be strong enough to try to seize the throne of Scotland.

DURING THOSE HEADY DAYS OF POTENTIAL KINGSHIP, HAY CREATED A HEROIC POEM IN STONE.

The building had a political purpose and, when it was completed, took on a life of its own in the public mind. The craftsmanship and skill in the use of stories and symbols that went into its construction has stood the test of time. Whatever William St Clair and Gilbert Hay had in mind when they cooperated in the design of the stone-work, surely they did not expect it to be a source of mythical inspiration for over half a millennium.

An immediate effect of the failure of William St Clair's coup was that construction at Roslin stopped and the masons were fired. William had accidentally created a workforce of skilled Scots masons by recruiting an international band of stoneworkers for a job that lasted the better part of 40 years. Many of them decided to seek work in Scotland rather than  return to the lands their fathers, or even grandfathers, had left four decades before.

If they wanted work in Scotland, Aberdeen was where the action was. St. Nicholas's Kirk was being extended by the Burgh Council. The Masons who moved to Aberdeen from Roslin had worked on a building whose stone-carved fabric provides the earliest evidence of what was to become Masonic ritual and symbolism. The group of former Roslin masons, led by David Menzies, drew these symbols on a ritual floorcloth to teach their meaning.

The newly redundant workers from Roslin were inspired by what they learned from Gilbert Hay's use of symbolism and mythical stories. After seeing him create a building with a powerful presence, they decided to study symbols and allegory themselves. They created a visual aid—now called the Kirkwall Scroll—and started to perform

rituals to explain the meaning of the symbols to their apprentices. Their startling success launched a worldwide spiritual self-help movement that has survived for over 600 years.

You can see the symbols they used by examining the Kirkwall Scroll. They based their allegorical stories on the construction of King Solomon's Temple as described in the Bible.

THE ORGANIZATION
OF FREEMASONRY

FROM THE VERY BEGINNING, the structure of Freemasonry has been hierarchical. The first lodge had a Master and two Wardens—a Senior Warden and a Junior Warden Over time, more officers were added to the structure, until seven officers were needed to form a lodge.

The lowest-ranking officer is the Outer Guard, who stands outside the lodge door with a drawn sword to prevent any unauthorized entries Next comes the Inner Guard, who stands inside the closed door of the

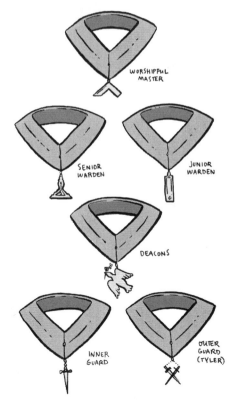

WORSHIPFUL MASTER

SENIOR WARDEN

JUNIOR WARDEN

DEACONS

INNER GUARD

OUTER GUARD (TYLER)

lodge holding a drawn dagger to stop anyone who might force his way past the Outer Guard. The Inner Guard is directed by the Junior Warden. Next up the scale is the Junior Deacon, who carries messages from the Senior Warden to the Junior Warden. Then there is the Senior Deacon, who carries the messages of the Master to the Senior Warden. Together these seven officers form the basic structure of the lodge. In order of seniority, from bottom to top, they are: Outer Guard (or

SENIOR DEACON

JUNIOR DEACON

OUTER GUARD (TYLER)

INNER GUARD

Tyler), Inner Guard, Junior Deacon, Senior Deacon, Junior Warden, Senior Warden, and, above everyone, Worshipful Master.

The Master commands the lodge and issues instructions to the rest of the lodge via the Wardens. The Master wields a small hammer, called a gavel, which he knocks to call for silence at meetings. Each of the Wardens also has a gavel, so when the Master knocks for silence before speaking, each of the Wardens also knocks. The sound of the knocks echoes around the lodge room. Only after the Master and two Wardens all have knocked, and the members of the lodge are silent, does the Master speak.

All officers of the lodge wear a collar, and from the collar hangs a badge to symbolize the wearer's office. For example, the badge for the Master has a set square, the Senior Warden a level, and the Junior Warden a plumb rule. These symbols are usually either made of silver or silver plate.

Rank Structure

Freemasonry's rank structure does not stop with the officers of the lodge. There is also a hierarchy among the ordinary members, with each wearing a different symbolic apron. When a new member is taken in, he or she becomes an Entered Apprentice.

They must serve some time learning ritual before they are ready to be promoted to the next rank—or degree, as Masons' say—which is that of Fellowcraft. An Entered Apprentice is not allowed to enter or remain inside a lodge that has been opened to carry out Fellowcraft, or second-degree, rituals. They must leave the lodge room and wait outside while the rituals of the Fellowcraft are being performed. The Outer Guard makes sure that that they do not eavesdrop on the proceedings. A Fellowcraft can enter or remain inside an Entered Apprentice's lodge, but when a Fellowcraft lodge is ritually opened as a Master Mason's Lodge, then the Fellowcrafts have to go outside and wait with the Apprentices.

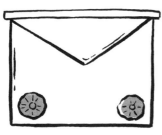

FELLOWCRAFT APRON

The apron worn by a Mason makes it easy to recognize their rank. The Fellowcraft's apron, like that of the Apprentice, is plain white and made of lambskin but decorated with two blue rosettes. The Master Mason's apron, which is also made of white lambskin, has a light blue border around the apron and its flap; it has the same two blue rosettes as that of a Fellowcraft, as well as a third blue rosette and two sets of silver tassels. In most systems of Freemasonry, the Worshipful Master wears an apron similar to that of

MASTER MASON'S APRON

WORSHIPFUL MASTER'S APRON

a Master Mason, but the three blue rosettes are replaced with three silver tee-squares. Once a Brother has served as the master of a lodge, he or she is called a Past Master and gets a light blue collar From this collar hangs a silver symbol showing the proof of the Pythagorean Theorem $(a^2 + b^2 = c^2)$ and a set square.

PAST MASTER'S COLLAR

FREEMASONRY KEEPS THE TEACHING OF ITS DEGREES SEPARATE.

This is to make sure that each new ritual a Candidate encounters when moving up to the next level has the maximum impact. No lower-ranking Freemason is allowed to take part in a lodge that is opened in a higher degree than the one they hold. As part of the ceremonies of promotion, they are given a special password and handgrip that allow them to enter "a lodge in a higher degree."

The four levels at which a lodge may be opened are:

- Entered Apprentice Lodge
- Fellowcraft Lodge
- Master Mason's Lodge
- Board of Installed Masters

Above the lodge, however, there are more levels of hierarchical organization. A group of lodges in a geographical province may join together to form a Provincial Grand Lodge, and all the Provincial Grand Lodges within a country form a Grand Lodge.

Grand and Provincial Grand Lodges

There are no Provincial Grand Lodges in the United States; instead, each state has its own Grand Lodge. In the United Kingdom, however, there are three male Grand Lodges and two female Grand Lodges; all of them have Provincial Grand Lodges underneath them.

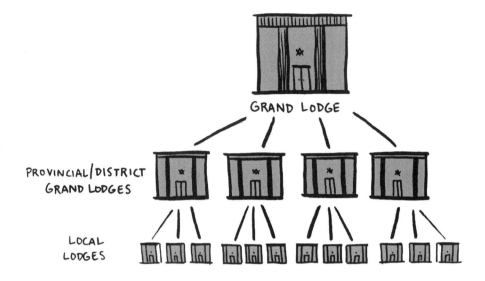

GRAND LODGE

PROVINCIAL/DISTRICT
GRAND LODGES

LOCAL
LODGES

The three older, male Grand Lodges in the UK are:

- The Grand Lodge of Scotland
- The Grand Lodge of England
- The Grand Lodge of Ireland

The Grand Lodge of Scotland has 32 provincial grand lodges and another 26 District Grand lodges, which look after Scottish Lodges set up in other parts of the world.

The Grand Lodge of England has 48 provinces, 33 overseas districts, and five smaller overseas groups.

The Grand Lodge of Ireland has 13 provinces in Ireland and 12 groups of overseas lodges. The latter include a special group of travelling military lodges, which are associated with Irish regiments wherever they are stationed.

There are a total of 93 Provincial Grand Lodges in the British Isles. Each one has a retinue of officers and ranks. For example, there are 58 ranks within an English Provincial Grand Lodge. These range from Provincial Grand Master to Provincial Grand Tyler. Each rank also has what are called Past Officers; these are like Past Masters, who held a rank in previous years.

The overall rank structure opens up a lot of opportunity to be promoted, and each promotion offers the chance to wear a more impressive apron. There is always something new to learn, and by continually undertaking new roles and being promoted to new offices within the Order, Freemasonry gives its members a motive to keep interested and continually learn new things.

BUT WHAT SORT of knowledge does Freemasonry teach its brethren? To understand that, we need to go back to where Freemasonry started and understand what the founding lodges intended to do. Fortunately, we can do that by looking at the symbols they studied and seeing how they are still taught through ritual performances.

THE RITUALS OF FREEMASONRY

NOBODY KNOWS MUCH ABOUT the rituals used by the early masters of the Lodge of Aberdeen, David Menzies, Matthew Wright, and Alexander Stuart, but we do know that they set about studying the power of symbols to affect the way people think. We know this because their early Masonic floorcloth, which shows all the symbols used in Freemasonry survives to the present day. It has been carbon dated to the 15th century, and its provenance has been traced to Aberdeen. There was no other lodge of Freemasons at the time, so we know they must have created it. But what inspired them to do something so new and

innovative in their little workshop alongside the partly built St Nicholas's Kirk?

To understand their inspiration, we need to remember that some of the early members and masters of the Lodge of Aberdeen had formerly worked on Rosslyn Chapel, farther to the south. There they had been exposed to the thinking of Sir Gilbert Hay, who had studied the use of symbols and buildings as tools of political influence. Hay had been set the task of creating an alternative center of spiritual focus to the Stuart king's Abbey of the True Cross, or Holyrood.

The Stuart dynasty of Scottish kings had used a holy relic to promote popular belief that their line had a Divine Right to rule. A fragment of the True Cross, they claimed, had protected King David I of Scotland from a rampaging stage. To house the relic, David created the Abbey of the Holyrood, and he encouraged the Scottish people to venerate its role in protecting the Stuart kings. The symbol of the Holyrood is a stag with the True Cross mounted in its antlers.

In the first half of the fifteenth century, when William St Clair, the baron of Roslin, decided to challenge the Stuarts for the crown of Scotland, he set about building a copy of King Solomon's Temple, the most famous building in the ancient world He intended it to be a spiritual focus for his coup d'état, and Gilbert Hay put a lot of time and effort into creating a building steeped in symbolism. To

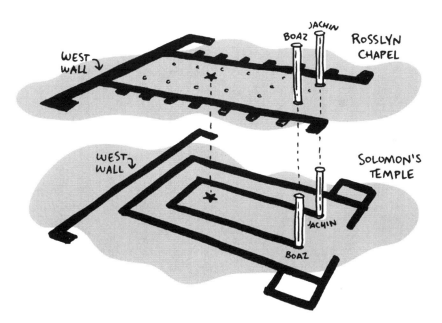

this day, the building creates a deep impression on anyone who visits. Hay set up a system of quality control for the stone carving and insisted that all symbols were first carved in wood and inspected by him before being cut into stone. The use of symbols impressed the stonemasons who worked for him. When the coup failed, the work-force was disbanded and left to find work elsewhere. The ones who ended up working on St. Nicholas's Kirk in Aberdeen took up the study of symbols and myths themselves.

These other paths of Freemasonry are available to members once they have completed the three degrees of the Craft. Examples include the Mark Degree, the Holy Royal Arch of Jerusalem, and the Masonic Knights Templar, among many others. Each side-order has its own rituals, which have been created to explain the symbols, but all of the symbols are contained on the first floorcloth. This means that the rit-uals came after the symbols. The rituals have been developed over a long period of time to help Masons understand the symbols.

They take their name from the white lambskin aprons, bordered with blue ribbon, worn by brethren. From contemporary writings, we know that the first lodge had only two rituals when it was formed: a ritual of entry for new members, known as Initiation; and a ritual to mark the point when an Apprentice had learned enough to become a Craftsman. Later they added a ceremony to mark the election of a new Master of the Lodge each year. Over time, these simple ceremonies grew to become the four Craft degrees in general use today: Entered Apprentice, Fellowcraft, Master Mason, and Installed Master.

Each ceremony teaches individual Masons something about themselves, something about society, and something about the ancient symbols. Even before you can be proposed as a Candidate for Freemasonry, however, you must meet certain ritual requirements.

To begin with, if you want to become a Freemason, you must "ask" to join. This means that you need to visit your local lodge and tell them you are interested in what they do. They are unlikely to ask you, though sometimes a Mason may ask a friend if they are interested. No one should ever be pressured to join the Masons. Anyone who is not interested in what Freemasonry does will not enjoy it and is unlikely to make a good lodge member.

If you do decide to visit your local Masonic Hall and ask about Freemasonry, the members will happily tell you about their lodge. They will encourage you to look around and ask about their activities. Many lodges have what they call "Gavel Nights," where members of the public are invited to see the lodge rooms and ask any questions they might have about Freemasonry.

Once you have found out a little more, and if you are still interested, you will be asked to come for an interview with a panel of senior members. They will want to determine if you will be a suitable Candidate. You will be asked if you believe in some form of Supreme Being. This is to find out if you think there is some form of basic order to the universe. If you don't think so, you will not be invited to seek membership. The reason for this is quite simple. The rituals of Freemasonry are designed to help members learn about themselves and the purpose of their lives. If you do not think there is any purpose to life, Freemasonry cannot help you. The panel will not ask if you follow any particular religion or creed, as…

Masonic rituals refer to a supreme source of order in the universe using names that are religiously neutral. Designations such as the Great Architect of the Universe or the Grand Geometrician of Universe are commonly used. Freemasonry does not allow discussion of religion and politics in the lodge. Its rituals bring together the common spiritual lessons of wide-ranging religious and scientific beliefs. To do this, it uses words intended to draw members together rather than force them apart. It seeks to build on the spiritual lessons shared by all faiths rather than dwell on issues of difference and conflict.

> **The rituals of Freemasonry have been developed to help members in two basic ways:**
>
> - To teach you about yourself, your motives, and your purpose in life.
> - To teach you about a series of ancient and powerful symbols that can deepen your understanding of the world you live in.

The First Degree

The ritual of the First Degree introduces prospective members to the idea that they must learn to face up to their fears and trust others to guide them when they cannot see their own way forward. As a Candidate, you are prepared to be made a Mason in the traditional way, according to ritual: you roll up your pants leg, expose your breast, and hang one shoe off your foot. As is widely rumored, you will also be blindfolded and have a hangman's noose placed round your neck. In some parts of the

world, you will be given a simple white suit to wear instead of your formal clothes. Anything valuable, such as watches, rings, and money, will be taken from you before you knock on the lodge door to ask admission.

The purpose of preparing prospective members in this way is to remove all external badges of rank and wealth. If a lodge is to let an individual join, it is because he or she has been judged to be a worthy person searching for Truth. No one is admitted because they are either rich or poor.

This is to demonstrate that the lodge values a person as a person, not because of their position in society or their material wealth.

Thus, the ritual of the First Degree strips you of all the normal trappings of wealth and power, such as fine clothing, expensive jewelry, and money. You are deprived of sight by means of a blindfold and led into a strange place where you cannot see what is going on. The first thing that happens when the door opens is that someone holds the sharp point of a dagger against your naked chest and asks if you can feel the point.

As the ceremony proceeds, you are guided by a hand on your arm and meet different individuals in different parts of the lodge who ask you questions about your motives and intentions. During the whole time, you are helped, prompted, and conducted around the lodge by a deacon who looks after your welfare. The deacon guides you as you walk and whispers in your ear what you need to do. A voice tells you that you will "pass in view before the brethren to show that you are a Candidate properly prepared to be made a Mason".

Finally, after you have freely agreed to accept the rules and guidance of the Order, your blindfold will be removed. Then you will be shown the main symbols of the lodge.

Now you have become a Brother Mason.

Next you will be taught how to identify yourself when you enter a lodge. You will be told the passwords of the degree and shown the ceremonial grips used during rituals. You will receive a number of short talks that counsel you to practice charity toward all in need. Just as you were admitted into the lodge "poor and penniless," so you should remember how this felt when you meet people in need.

You will be told the three main principles of Freemasonry:

These ideals are referred to in short as Brotherly Love, Relief, and Truth.

During the initiation ceremony, you will have been taught to face up to your fears; to learn to trust your guides within Freemasonry; and to understand that you can overcome your fears if you do stand up to them. This constitutes the first lesson in understanding yourself and the deeper meaning of life.

You will also have been told about the value of keeping a good work/life balance; about the need to study and do your best to become as well-educated as you can; and to listen to the small, inner voice of your conscience so that you behave well in all situations.

And you will have been warned that you must commit some key pieces of ritual to memory before you can be admitted to the next degree. These bits of ritual will be acted out for you to see, and you will be assigned a mentor to help you memorize and practice your part.

Because you will have been exposed to a lot of ideas and information in a short period of time, you will probably be quite confused.

The Second Degree

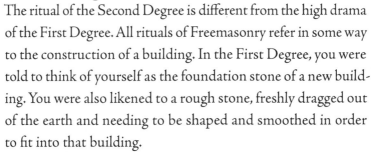

The ritual of the Second Degree is different from the high drama of the First Degree. All rituals of Freemasonry refer in some way to the construction of a building. In the First Degree, you were told to think of yourself as the foundation stone of a new building. You were also likened to a rough stone, freshly dragged out of the earth and needing to be shaped and smoothed in order to fit into that building.

There are two ways to think about this symbolism. The message that you are a rough stone that has to be shaped in order to fit into society is one way of looking at it. But what about that strange moment when you are told to think of yourself as a foundation stone of a new building? The new building represents your personality, which you are being encouraged to develop by thinking about the benefits of education and leading a moral and responsible life.

Whenever Freemasonry talks about a building, it regards it as a symbol of individual personality or character. In the First Degree, you are encouraged to lay a foundation based on sound morals and the desire to learn more. The Second Degree helps you to develop your mind and teaches ways to think about the wonders of the world in which you live.

If the ground floor was based on learning to tackle difficult issues and do what's right, the second floor introduces a vast library of knowledge about the natural world.

Before you can be admitted to the Second Degree, you must prove that you have applied yourself to the lessons of the First Degree. You will have had to learn a series of ritual questions and answers. In this way, Masonic teaching often takes the form of a catechism. This is a sequence of formal questions and answers that Candidates have to learn by heart and answer in the open lodge. This develops the memory to an amazing extent.

Once you have been tested in the catechism, the brethren will vote on whether your recital was good enough to award you the higher degree. Once they decide you have learned the lessons of the previous degree, you will be taken outside and once again stripped of all your valuables and badges of rank and privilege. As you leave the lodge, you will be given a password to memorize. You will be required to recite the password before being allowed back into the lodge, which by then will have been opened as a Fellowcraft lodge.

Once you give the password, you will be paraded around the lodge once again—this time with your eyes open—to show the brethren that you are still poor and penniless. This is an important symbolic moment, as it demonstrates to you that you are being promoted because of your personality, not because of any wealth or status.

Once you have promised to accept the teachings of the Fellowcraft degree and keep secret its means of identification, you will be taught how to identify yourself using the ritual grips and passwords. These are formal ways of proving yourself a Fellowcraft that are used only inside the lodge.

Ritually, meanwhile, you are working on the construction of the second story of the building that is your character. You will act out the climbing of stairs to reach the second level, where you will be told that it is now your duty to study "the hidden mysteries of nature and science" in order that you might better understand the world you live in.

The ritual of the Second Degree has inspired many scientists over the years. Brothers Enrico Fermi (physics), Alexander Fleming (medicine), and Edward Appleton (physics) were Freemasons who also won Nobel Prizes for their devoted study of nature and science. James Watt, the inventor of the steam engine; George and Robert Steven-

son, the inventors of the steam railway; Edward Jenner; the discoverer of the smallpox vaccine; and William and Charles Mayo, founders of the Mayo Clinic, all were Fellowcraft Masons. Countless other scientific researchers, including many founders of Britain's Royal Society, have been inspired by this second degree of Freemasonry.

In the Second Degree, members are given mental tools—based on physical ones used by stonemasons—that enable them to determine the three dimensions of space. In combination with the time measurement techniques of the First Degree, they have been given all the mental tools that Albert Einstein had when he developed the Theory of Relativity

In the Second Degree, you are also given a hint that there is a mysterious symbol at the center of the building you are erecting. This suggests a deep truth hidden within you—though that will have to wait until you take your Third Degree. Before then, you will be required to learn a formal set of questions and answers as preparation.

The Third Degree

You begin by being tested in the ritual catechism. If the members juvdge you to have done well in what Freemasonry calls "the Art of Memory," you will be allowed to take the Third Degree. You will be sent out of the lodge to remove your wealth and rank, and to be given another password. Reciting the new password will allow you back into the lodge once it is opened for Master Masons.

The Third Degree is a serious and somber ritual designed to make Candidates realize that they, like everyone else, will die. Its purpose is to encourage them to make good use of the time they are alive.

In this ritual, Candidates act out an ancient legend about one of the senior supervisors who worked on King Solomon's Temple. This famous Masonic character, from the Old Testament, was the son of widow and a skilled craftsman. He was able to create beautiful buildings. He worked with King Solomon, who had the inspiration to build a great temple, and King Hiram of Tyre, who provided all the materials that were needed. In addition, this Masonic hero had to organize

his workers to assemble all the raw materials into the most beautiful building in the world.

How he managed to create such a beautiful building—a symbol of character—was a secret known only to him and his two construction bosses, King Solomon of Israel and King Hiram of Tyre. However, he did tell his workmen that he would share the secret with them when he thought they were ready.

The story is set at the time when King Solomon's Temple was nearly finished. Some of the more impatient workmen, desperate to know his secret techniques, decided to try to force him to tell. They waited until the noonday meal break, when they knew he would be on his own. He always sought out a quiet moment to pray and reflect

on what he still had to do within the partly built temple. They knew he would be alone and unprotected.

At first it looked as if many other workmen would join in the attempt to force their supervisor to share his construction knowledge. In the end, only three were willing to go to such extremes. Sometime before

noon on the appointed day, each of the three ruffians went to a different temple entrance and waited for the supervisor to emerge. The three gates are said to represent the different aspects of one's lower nature that are needed to build a better character. The first two ruffians, symbolizing fear and intellectual arrogance, succeeded only in wounding the supervisor. He refused to give up his secrets. The third ruffian, representing the ego that does not believe it will ever die, then killed the supervisor.

The rest of the Third Degree ritual shows what it would be like to attend your own funeral and forces you to think about the fact of your own mortality. Then the master of the lodge lifts you out of your despair and welcomes you back to the rest of your life. The master reminds you that life is fleeting and a gift that you should make the most of.

But there is more. The ritual also points out that there is a purpose in life. To find it, you must work with the rest of society to seek out Wisdom, Truth, and Beauty. These are what give life purpose. At the center of yourself, you are told, is a Divine Spark that connects you to the whole of Creation. The purpose of life is to discover and understand how to use the Divine Spark of Consciousness to help you become a better person. This will also help you make society a better place to live.

At its heart, the message of Freemasonry is hope and toleration. It recognizes and accepts that all religions, as well as many branches of science, find a wonderful mystery in human consciousness and a relationship to the cosmos that gives life purpose. All of modern science is based on the idea that there is order at the heart of creation and that it is worthy of study. A scientist may call it the Laws of Physics, a Christian may call it The Trinity, a Jew may call it Yahweh, and a Muslim may call it Allah. All accept there is a marvelous source of order at the center of creation that one can spend a lifetime studying.

Freemasonry uses myths and symbolical language to enable people of all beliefs to come together and share their insights rather than argue about their differences. It employs neutral terms such as the Great Architect of the Universe so as not to bias the message. To avoid conflict, Freemasonry forbids the discussion of religion or politics, but

it encourages members to share their inner sacred feelings and work together to help one another understand the nature of the cosmos.

Masonic rituals encourage members to act out basic lessons so they experience the things they want to learn about. They learn how to face up to, and overcome, their fears. They learn how to develop their mind and intellect. And finally, they learn how to come to terms with their mortality.

The biblical story of the building of King Solomon's Temple is used as a symbol of the mental work needed to build a wise, beautiful, and strong personality. Freemasonry aims to take good people and make them better, and it does this by helping them grow and develop. It is the oldest spiritual self-help society in the Western world. It has survived and thrived since those first stumbling attempts by inspired individuals to improve themselves and their society in the late 15th century.

THE SYMBOLS OF FREEMASONRY

IF YOU ASK ANY MASON "What is Freemasonry?" they will answer with the automatic, ritual reply: *"a peculiar system of morality veiled in allegory and illustrated by symbols."* But what does this mean? In previous chapters, we looked at the ways in which Freemasonry uses allegory, myth, and ritual. Now we will look at what it teaches about symbols.

Until recently in human history, only a few individuals have recognized the importance of symbols in the way societies work. Yet one group has received centuries of extensive train-ing in the use and power of symbols and has been taught how to understand the energy that can flow from the display of symbols in public places. They know that understanding symbols is an ancient skill that most humans

are born with and that the influence of some symbols on human actions is universal.

In the early years of the 21st century, popular fiction latched onto this idea. It became the subject of some extremely successful thrillers, such as *The Da Vinci Code* by Dan Brown, which drew on books about the underground stream of Masonic symbolism. Brown's follow-up novel, *The Lost Symbol* (2009), took as its main theme the search for a great Masonic symbol of power.

One group in particular thinks they do. For them, the study of symbols is an important part of life. Perhaps it is a coincidence, but many members of this group have become prominent figures in the history of humanity. They helped invent modern science. They helped forged the republics that brought freedom to the masses. They have been at the forefront of scientific development. They have been influential writers, musicians, industrialists, astronauts, and politicians. And what they have in common is Freemasonry. All have been part of an order that has spent the last six centuries studying the way symbols and people interact to bring about progress or disaster.

Types of Symbols

Symbols speak to us at a deeper level than writing. The primary ideas of Masonic teaching are deeply rooted in the use of symbols. Some of

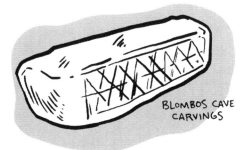

BLOMBOS CAVE
CARVINGS

these symbols date back to the first attempts by humans to scratch shapes into stone more than 70,000 years ago. And some of the symbols drawn by our ancient ancestors are still in use today. Many people wear them on their clothes and display them on their cars. Such primeval symbols transcend all disparities in human language.

Symbols first meshed with rituals in the shamanistic cave paintings of North Europe about 30,000 years ago. Used to promote hunting in pre-farming days, they were considered essential to survival.

By the 17th century, symbolism was being employed in two ways. First, loosely defined symbols were used to create images, emotions, and feelings in a ritual context. This is the essential idea used in modern visual advertising. The other purpose was to help the human mind to reason and develop a deeper grasp of the world.

To understand how this happened, you need to know that there are three main types of symbols:

Emotive Symbols, which encode feelings and aspirations. These are the oldest of all symbols, dating back 70,000 years, and they have been widely used in history to evoke emotion in illiterate people.

Speech Symbols, which encode the sounds of language in alphabets or pictograms. They enable humans to communicate across time and space. At one time, these symbols were tightly restricted to elite groups, often linked to a religion.

Mathematical Symbols, which encode the means of understanding and predicting reality. Freemasons helped develop algebra and calculus, the building blocks of modern analytical mathematics.

For nearly 2,500 years, since the time of the Greek philosopher Plato, some individuals have believed that there is a realm of perfect symbols. They maintain that, with careful training, anyone can be taught how to communicate with this realm and thereby discover the true nature of these perfect symbols.

Since its origin, Freemasonry has relied on symbols as a unique, universal language to share its ideas. One key reason is that an idea expressed in symbols can be spread without corruption. This assures continuity of tradition. Modern Masons carry out their symbolic work in exactly the same way as a Mason of 500 years ago. Today's Mason faces the same problems that a Mason living in the 15th century faced. And the symbols provide eternally truthful answers.

The Masonic Symbols

About 60 basic symbols are taught to aspiring Masters as they progress through the degrees of Freemasonry. The symbols are introduced as a new member moves through the degrees of the Craft, the Mark, and the Royal Arch. Eventually they are combined into pictorial narratives called **Tracing Boards**. There are four main Tracing Boards, each of which conveys a different philosophical message.

Freemasonry's way of teaching symbolism is called "illumination by symbols." This method has had a powerful influence on notable individuals and events in Western history.

Q. Why do all U.S. presidents make a Masonic sign during inauguration ceremonies?

• A. Because George Washington was a Freemason, he brought several items of Masonic symbolism to his first inauguration. As he stood before the new flag of the United States, he made the Masonic sign of fidelity, covering his heart with his right palm, as a gesture of fidelity. He also took the oath of office on the Volume of the Sacred Law, borrowed from St. John's Lodge in New York. These symbols did, and still do, make the ceremony a more emotionally powerful event for the audience.

Oliver Cromwell, the first Lord Protector of the Republican Commonwealth of Great Britain in the 1650s, had himself portrayed standing between the two porch pillars of Freemasonry. The Masonically inspired French Revolution took as its inspiration the great tripartite motto "Liberty, Equality, Fraternity,"

BENJAMIN FRANKLIN

a set of symbolic names given to the three working pillars of a Masonic Lodge (often identified as Doric, Ionic, and Corinthian). The great outcry of the American Revolution, "No taxation, without representation," was coined by the brethren of St. Andrews Lodge in Boston. It became the spark that kindled the greatest Masonic document of all times, the American Constitution. And the very impetus for a written constitution for the new United States came in large part from Bro. (Brother) Ben Franklin.

FOR OVER 500 YEARS, THE SYMBOLOGY OF FREEMASONRY HAS FOSTERED A SECRET STREAM OF RADICAL IDEAS BENEATH THE SURFACE OF POPULAR CULTURE.

These powerful concepts, illuminated by public symbols hidden in full view, have influenced and shaped the society in which we live.

The first Freemasons were 15th-century stoneworkers, employed to carve symbols of religious significance into public places of worship. They recognized the power of these symbols and realized that shapes could influence people's thoughts and actions. This is why they decided to study ancient symbols and learn how they affected human thought. They understood that a symbol is a pictorial device that can evoke a concept in its entirety. A symbol bypasses the intellect and speaks straight to the heart. The intellect analyses, but the heart synthesizes. A symbol evokes understanding and feeling without needing to convey verbal information.

Understanding Symbols

Carl Gustav Jung, the famous Swiss psychologist, said that symbols speak to us of "things beyond the range of human understanding." They tap into a source of knowledge that is not normally open to the conscious mind. Jung defined these symbols as "a term, a name or an image that may be familiar in daily life, yet ... possesses specific connotations in addition to its conventional meanings and implies some-

CARL JUNG

thing vague, unknown or hidden from us."

He pointed out that when your mind explores the symbol it is led to ideas that lie beyond the grasp of reason. Because many phenomena and experiences lie beyond the range of human understanding, we constantly use symbolic terms to represent the things we cannot fully comprehend.

According to the Greek philosopher Plato, symbols represent a transcendental world of perfect and beautiful forms that can be reached only by the human soul. The most vital human knowledge, which derives from the world of forms, is recalled by the human soul from before physical birth.

While we have no difficulty in deciding whether or not two people are equal in height, they are never exactly the same. We can always discover a minute difference by making a more careful measurement. This means that all the examples of equality we recognize in ordinary life can only approach, but never quite reach, the state of perfect equality. At the same time, we recognize Truth from our experience. Somehow we know what true equality is, even though we can't measure it.

Plato's ideas inspired the Masonic teaching that the world is essentially intelligible. Our intellect, not our senses, has the ultimate "vision" of true being. Freemasons learn to understand the world from the deep knowledge that is conveyed to the heart through symbols.

Both Plato and Jung are talking about a reality that lies beyond normal human consciousness and can be reached only through symbols.

Symbolic knowledge thus has a spiritual or transcendental dimension. That is why it has been the subject of Masonic study and teaching over the centuries.

TO SEE IF these ancient symbols are still active in the minds of modern humans, I—the author of this book—conducted a series of tests on volunteer students to see how they responded. I used a technique called Galvanic Skin Response (GSR), which measures the degree of emotional arousal caused by visual, verbal, or other stimuli. Used in polygraphs (lie detectors) and other biofeedback devices, it relies on the fact that people have little control over what makes them sweat. Sweat is a good conductor of electricity, making it possible to detect and gauge emotional impact.

With this built-in physiological indicator of emotional impact, I was able to study how people from different backgrounds reacted to

my chosen symbols. With access to student volunteers from around the world, I was able to test individuals who had been brought up in British, African, Asian, American, European, and Chinese cultures and had been taught to read in different writing systems, using different methods of recording words, and speaking different mother tongues. I tested equal numbers of females and males in each culture/alphabet group and repeated the procedure over a number of years.

The objects of study were twelve shapes—six from modern jewelry and six ancient symbols. I chose modern jewelry because its decorative motifs are designed to appeal to people today.

The results were consistent. Viewing the ancient symbols caused an unfailing change in galvanic skin response, while responses to the modern jewelry shapes were more varied.

One thing I could not tell was whether the responses to the ancient symbols were positive or negative. Did my students like these symbols or find them disturbing?

As the responses were visceral and sub-

conscious, there was little point in querying the subjects how they felt about the images. When I did try asking, they struggled to artic-ulate their feelings. The only sure way to find out was to conduct a follow-up survey with the same subjects, asking different questions about the symbols. So I asked them to rank the same set of images in terms of attractiveness.

The results were telling. The highest-ranked images were the ones that had caused significant GSR responses. The perspiration I had measured was the glow of pleasure, not the cold sweat of fear.

BETTY EDWARDS

PROFESSOR BETTY EDWARDS, who taught art California State University, Long Beach, and wrote the bestselling book *Drawing on the Right Side of the Brain* (1979), observed how students found consistent meaning in certain drawings. They reached a point in training, she noted, that "meaning is expressed in a parallel visual language of a drawing, whether it represents recognizable objects or is completely non-objective. A drawing, to be comprehended for meaning, must be read by means of the language used by the artist, and that meaning, once comprehended, may be beyond the power of words to express. Yet in its parts and as a whole, it can be read."

Parts of the human brain have evolved to look at abstract shapes and relate to the emotions and thoughts that were in the mind of the person who drew them. Sensitivity to the emotive message of symbols is innate, but it can be enhanced through training. The ability to interact with symbols makes humans different from other animals. Freemasonry's study of these ancient, transcendental symbols has led to momentous breakthroughs in diverse areas of endeavor.

Writing is one special form of symbolic magic. It enables people to converse with a friend in a distant country and instantly absorb the reply. It lets a deceased relative recount personal experiences that they would never talk about when alive. It lets the long-dead inhabitants of the ancient cities of Sumer, in Mesopotamia, continue to tell the story of their first king, Gilgamesh.

Because the first Freemasons in Aberdeen did not know how to read, they developed a verbal way of teaching symbols to commit their knowledge to memory. The symbols they studied were initially drawn on the floor of the lodge in chalk and then mopped up after the meeting ended. Later they were painted on a canvas carpet. One such carpet has survived as the Kirkwall Scroll.

Indeed, for the first few hundred years of its existence, Freemasonry distrusted written language. Passing on its knowledge using emotive symbols and poetic metaphor had the beneficial side effect of training memory. So Freemasonry came to value "The Art of Memory."

Human consciousness

CARRIES out two kinds of functions. For delicate tasks, the brain focuses its attention narrowly—to pick up a grain of corn instead of a piece of stone that lies next to it, for example. But human consciousness must also maintain a wide field of attention, particularly to remain aware of predators. A person who couldn't concentrate could starve; a person who couldn't remain alert could get killed and eaten. This is why humans evolved "two brains," corresponding to functions controlled by each hemisphere. The left brain concentrates on detailed tasks and is language-driven. The right brain takes a wider overview and uses symbols to compress information about surroundings. This evolutionary quirk has given humans two essential thinking systems— one that chatters and one that responds to symbols.

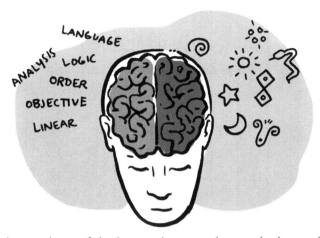

Each hemisphere of the human brain understands the world in a different way. The left brain does not understand metaphor, narrative, or emotive symbols. We listen to stories, visualize symbols, and react emotionally to images using our inarticulate right brain. The left brain focuses attention narrowly; it concentrates. The right brain stays alert to what is happening all around you. The left brain sees bits of the world but has trouble linking them together. The right brain recognizes meaning in symbols and sees connections. The emotional response to ancient symbols takes place in the right hemisphere, while the left brain enables us concentrate on a topic of interest and ignore everything on the outside. Thus we can attach meaning to symbols that we can't put into words.

It is worth noting at this point that the function of the corpus callosum, the wiring that connects the two hemispheres, is not really to communicate information between them. Neurologically, its purpose is to inhibit one or other of the hemispheres from acting. The evolutionary advantage of the human split brain stems from this fact: If the right brain perceives a threat, it can "turn off" the focused attention of the left brain and force us to become aware of our surroundings and, perhaps, avoid being eaten by predators. Likewise, the left brain can stop the right hemisphere from indulging its curiosity about everything around it and force us to focus on tasks needed to stay alive. Thus, when we try to use words to explain symbols, we encourage our left hemisphere to inhibit the right. This was why my students were not able to explain how the symbols affected them even though they consistently spotted the ones with a powerful emotional message.

The Symbols of Science

$$F = G \frac{m_1 m_2}{r^2}$$

$$R_{\mu\nu} - \frac{1}{2} R g_{\mu\nu} = 8\pi G T_{\mu\nu}$$

$$i\hbar \frac{\partial}{\partial t} \Psi(r, t) = \hat{H} \Psi(r, t)$$

Soon after the Restoration of the British monarchy in 1660, a group of Freemasons tapped into a completely new set of symbols. The Masons had already been sensitized to the import of symbols through their ritual training, but this new group of symbols unleashed a power that could destroy the world. They were the words of a great cosmic language.

The English Civil War began as an argument between the king and his Parliament. It ended with the public beheading of King Charles I in 1649. In the midst of the bitter battles between king and Parliament, the symbols of modern mathematical science appeared How did a superstitious country, which burned alive at least 100 elderly women each year on suspicion of causing disease by casting the "evil eye," suddenly develop a critical mass of discerning, mathematical scientists? How did they become adept, so quickly, in the symbols of science?

It didn't happen by chance. A symbol already used by Masons to stand for Equality and Balance, rotated through "an angle of ninety degrees, or the fourth part of circle," took on a whole new meaning.

This insight began in London, at Gresham College, on November 28, 1660. After a public lecture by scientist and architect Christopher Wren, the first meeting of what would become the Royal Society was convened. Sir Robert Moray, a Freemason whose story we will look at later, brought together a group of fellow Masons who were already alert to the meaning of symbols. As Masons, they were also inspired to study "the hidden mysteries of nature and science." These two aspects of their background proved to be a formidable combination.

Sir Robert's aim was to get the Brethren to work together to solve the problems of geometry and military construction to strengthen King Charles II's weak navy. He did this despite the fact that they came from both sides of the recent Civil War. Moray offered the Masons an opportunity to study interesting problems and earn the favor of the restored Stuart king. In the end, however, Moray achieved far more than restoring the British Navy. His new Royal Society made use of a group of symbols that enabled them to read and understand the plans of the Great Architect of the Universe.

John Wallis, who discovered this family of symbols, wrote about his links to the Craft and its role in the early meetings of the Royal Society. He reported that Masonic meetings had helped him recognize the latent power in the symbols of mathematics. Wallis, who became Savilian Professor of Geometry at Oxford in 1649, recognized that symbols could be made to stand in for real things and that they could then be manipulated to predict events in the real world. He passed on this knowledge to his brethren in the Royal Society, as well as his students, opening up a whole new range of opportunities.

"Mathematics were scarce looked on as academical studies," Wallis wrote, "but rather as the business of traders, merchants, seamen, carpenters, surveyors of lands and the like."

He had been shown the power of representative symbols by Freemason and astrologer William Oughtred, the inventor the slide rule. (The slide rule reduces multiplication and division to a simple mechanical manipulation of number positions on a linear scale. It made it simple to calculate the positions of the stars when casting a horoscope.)

As a student, Wallis lived in Oughtred's house in Albury, Surrey, and then went to Cambridge to become a Fellow of Queen's College. He later moved to London to become secretary to the clergy of

Westminster Abbey, where he renewed his friendship with his old tutor and met Oughtred's fellow Freemasons. In those early Masonic meetings, he found men who shared his interests and guided him toward a deeper understanding of symbols.

There is a fundamental mystery to the simple algebraic equations that we learn in school. Albert Einstein was so impressed by the theory of equations and the worlds they opened that he remarked, "I am in the position of a little child entering a huge library filled with books in many languages. I know someone must have written those books. I do not know how. I do not understand the languages but I dimly suspect a mysterious order in the arrangements of the books. I see a universe marvellously arranging and obeying certain laws, but only dimly understand these laws."

THE SYMBOLIC POWER of equations derives from two key factors:

A symbol can be used to represent something real, such as the speed of a stone falling to the ground or the number of gulps of trapped air a man can take in a diving bell without running out of oxygen. (These were actual problems considered by members of the early Royal Society).

The correspondence of the two sides of an equation is total, absolute, and uncompromising.

WHEN JOHN WALLIS discovered the full power of the equation, his Masonic training had sensitized him to the idea that the "=" symbol looks like two pillars "‖" laid horizontally on a level and meaning "is equal to." The Masonic ritual, Wallis would have learned, says the following about the symbolism the Level (tool):

> *The Level is to lay levels, and prove horizontals. ...*
> *The Level demonstrates that we are all sprung from*
> *the same stock, partakers of the same nature, and*
> *sharers in the same hope; and although distinctions*
> *among men are necessary to preserve subordination, yet*
> *ought no eminence of situation make us forget that we*
> *are Brothers; for he who is placed on the lowest spoke*
> *of fortune's wheel is equally entitled to our regard; as*
> *a time will come and the wisest of us knows not how*
> *soon when all distinctions, save those of goodness*
> *and virtue, shall cease, and Death, the grand leveller*
> *of all human greatness, reduces us to the same state. ...*
> *The Level teaches equality.*

When moving from the degree of an Apprentice to that of a Fellowcraft, Wallis would have first had to acknowledge the power of another symbol. The ritual goes as follows:

Further, Wallis would have recognized both the level and the rotation of the fourth part of a circle. The combination of these symbols gave him a great insight. Sir Isaac Newton, who discovered the law of gravity, was inspired by Wallis to think about symbolic reasoning. After Newton met Wallis, he took a special interest in Solomon's Temple; indeed he wrote more unpublished notes about that building than he did about mathematics or science. Solomon's Temple is an object of special interest to Freemasons for its use in teaching and sensitizing brethren to the hidden meaning of symbols and the power of buildings as analogs of human character.

Newton's work on equations extended Wallis's use of the equals sign, published in a book called *Arithmetica Universalis* (*Universal Arithmetic*) in 1707. Some 15 years earlier, Newton had written a number of letters to Wallis with his ideas about a new form of symbolic representation that became his greatest work on the reality of nature. The method is known as the calculus. It combines the pictorial visualization system of Euclid with Wallis's representation of physical quantities as algebraic symbols.

Newton used the Masonic idea of god as the Grand Geometrician of the Universe to bring Euclid's system of graphic symbols together with the mathematical analysis made possible by algebraic symbols. He published his work in 1687 as *Philosophiae Naturalis Principia Mathematica* (Mathematical Principles of Natural Philosophy). The *Principia* was a landmark step toward a modern understanding of the universe According to the *Stanford Encyclopaedia of Philosophy*, "No work was  more seminal in the development of modern physics and astronomy than Newton's *Principia*."

Newton's understanding had derived in large part from his exposure to Masonic symbolism. The innate power of these symbols is seen in the way Masonic knowledge affected the thinking of others when Newton shared it. While the dispute between the German philosopher Gottfried Leibniz and Isaac Newton over who discovered the calculus first is well known, what is less well known is that both Newton and Leibniz were exposed to the same symbolic teaching by Freemasons of the Royal Society—Newton through his associations with Wallis and Oughtred and his readings of astrologer William Lilly, and Leibniz through a long correspondence with Bro. Sir Robert Moray. The unique symbolic mix of geometric insight and algebraic analysis that is the calculus appeared simultaneously to these two men as if it had been fully formed form in another place and was just waiting for a chance to make itself known.

Masonry's Platonic View of Symbols

Masonic teaching offers a way of accessing a mental realm where

symbols are eternally present. Even some physicists refer to this realm as "Platonic heaven," derived from Plato's philosophy of the perfect forms. Sir Roger Penrose, the modern British physicist and a committed scientific Platonist, says, "The Platonic viewpoint is an immensely valuable one. It tells us to be careful to distinguish precise mathematical entities from the approximations that we see around us in the world of physical things."

The Platonist idea of eternal and perfect symbols underlies the modern scientific method of answering questions about reality. It gives rise to the term "re-search." A scientist conducts research by repeating a search—as any individual can—to discover a truth about the nature of reality that is open to any person prepared to access the Platonic symbols.

World War II provides a striking example of the Masonic idea regarding the power of symbols. Leo Szilard, Albert Einstein, and Niels Bohr, all physicists working for the Allies, realized that a weapon of immense destructive power existed in the realm of symbolic Platonic Truth. As they viewed the situation, a frightful weapon powerful enough to win the war was just waiting for the first bold searcher to reach out and acquire it. Success could come from either side, as basic work on nuclear power had been carried out by German scientists as well. There was great fear that this fearsome weapon was sitting unprotected, as it were, in the heaven of the Platonic symbols waiting to be accessed and put to use.

In August 1939, Szilard and Einstein sent a letter to President Franklin Roosevelt urging him to devote the nation's scientific talent and resources to searching for the atom bomb. The consequences of Hitler getting to it first, they warned, would be catastrophic. Roosevelt, himself a Freemason, took their warning seriously and launched the Manhattan Project. The rest is history.

FREEMASONRY'S WAY OF teaching is to display a symbol as part of the lodge's decoration, by wearing it as badge or a token, or by drawing it on a Tracing Board. When a junior Mason is shown the symbol, ritual statements are made about it that help the Brother understand its purpose and become sensitized to its emotional power. Ritual poetry, further sensitizing each Candidate to the power of the symbol, is committed to memory and recited by heart. With the introduction of each symbol to a new Freemason, a series of poetic ritual statements are made about its purpose and function, teaching the Brother how to apply the emotional import of the symbol to his or her own soul. The ritual description is memorized and repeated while the Brother looks at the image.

All in all, the Masonic method has proved to be a powerful way of learning about symbols.

FREEMASONRY AND RELIGION

FREEMASONRY IS NOT A RELIGION. Rather, it is a tolerant philosophy that welcomes people of any religious belief. It helps them share the things they hold in common rather than argue about their differences. To avoid sectarian disputes, it forbids talk of politics and religion in its lodges. It teaches a neutral language to explore the spiritual sensibilities that are common to all religious traditions, using such terms as the Great Architect of the

Universe and the Grand Geometrician of the Universe. Its spiritual training rituals are compatible with the belief systems of any religion, while also consistent with the rational worldview of science.

To join Freemasonry, a person must be able to express a belief that there is some order underpinning the behavior of the universe. If you are interested in joining a lodge, make sure you accept this view. Freemasonry is a spiritual path to help individuals join with fellow human beings who think that life has some sort of purpose. If you think life is purposeless, then Freemasonry has nothing to offer you, and you have nothing to offer Freemasonry.

Followers of the major world religions credit the source of order in the universe to their respective god or gods, but every physicist believes in sure and certain laws that determine the basis of reality. One can hardly become a physicist without believing that there are basic laws to be found. This faith is just as powerful and carries a sense of purpose as great as that held by the follower of any religion.

Your Supreme Being

Freemasonry's teachings can provide a focal point for people who have believe in some form of supreme order but are not active in any particular faith. They might see it as a stand-in for organized religion, as it provides spiritual values without the obligation to subscribe to an entire belief system. It is tolerant in a way that most religions are not, and its symbolic teachings are open to a range of interpretations that embrace people of all beliefs. It allows them to take what they need from the system and so learn more about themselves and how to meet their spiritual needs.

I am a physicist who was brought up in the Presbyterian tradition. It was only when I first asked to join a lodge that I had to think hard about what I believed. My proposer into Freemasonry took me to one side as I was about to give him my application form.

That was the moment I had to examine my scientific beliefs. Because the question seemed ambiguous, I ended up doing considerable research to decide how to answer. I began by looking at the meanings of the words used.

According to the *Concise Oxford Dictionary*, **"being"** is defined as: *existence, the nature or essence of, a human being, anything that exists or is imagined.*

"Supreme" is defined as: *highest in authority, greatest, most important, involving death, a rich cream sauce, a dish in this sauce.*

Thus, while the term **"supreme being"** is often taken as a synonym for God, the dictionary suggest wider possibilities. For example, a person could legitimately join the Masons if he or she believes in a deity who, though limited in power, is made of a rich cream sauce. (Let's call this hypothetical Supreme Being the "custard god.") When I first realized the possibility of this definition, I wondered if this might be why Freemasonry is sometimes called "the belly club"—William

Hogarth's well-known series of 18th-century etchings showing the Freemason with a distended belly still haunts many a Festive Board. But a custard god is simply too silly or too weird for a serious scientist to accept. Luckily, the phrase "supreme being" can also mean the greatest nature or essence of existence that can be imagined—which I understand to be the Laws of Physics.

As a physicist, I fully accept the concept of Supreme Being as put forward in 1725 by Sir Isaac Newton in *Principia Mathematica:*

The most beautiful system of the sun, planets, and comets, could only proceed from the counsel and dominion of an intelligent and powerful being. And if the fixed stars are the centres of like systems, these, being formed by the like wise counsel, must be all subject to the dominion of one; especially since the light of the fixed stars is of the same nature with the light of the sun, and from every system light passes into all the other systems; and lest the systems of fixed stars should, by their gravity, fall on each other, he hath placed those systems at immense distances from one another. The Supreme Being is eternal, infinite, absolutely perfect, omnipotent and omniscient. We know him only by his most wise and excellent contrivances of things and final causes.

When I showed this definition of Supreme Being to my proposer, his response surprised me.

He then repeated something that I later learned was a piece of Masonic ritual:

No one truly obeys the Masonic law who merely tolerates those whose religious opinions are opposed to their own. Every one's opinions are their own private property, and the rights of all people to maintain their own are perfectly equal. Merely to tolerate, to bear with an opposing opinion, is to assume it to be heretical, and assert the right to persecute, if we would, and claim our toleration as a merit. The Mason's creed goes further than that; no one, has any right, in any way, to interfere with the religious belief of another. It holds that everyone is absolutely sovereign as to his own belief, and that belief is a matter absolutely foreign to all who do not entertain the same belief; and that if there is any right of persecution at all, it will in all cases be a mutual right, because any party only has the same right as any other to sit as judge in their own case not on that of anyone else's.

Here is a statement of supreme tolerance. It requires only that the individual asking for membership in Freemasonry seeks to understand his or her own place in the greater system of the Universe. And if the purpose of religion is to help followers understand their place in the Cosmos, science has the same goal. In 1949, Albert Einstein wrote:

> You will hardly find one among the profounder sort of scientific minds without a peculiar religious feeling of his own. But it is different from the religion of the naive man. For the latter, God is a being from whose care one hopes to benefit and whose punishment one fears; a sublimation of a feeling similar to that of a child for its father, a being to whom one stands to some extent in a personal relation, however deeply it may be tinged with awe. But the scientist is possessed by the sense of universal causation. The future, to him, is every whit as necessary and determined as the past. There is nothing divine about morality, it is a purely human affair. His religious feeling takes the form of a rapturous amazement at the harmony of natural law, which reveals an intelligence of such superiority that, compared with it, all the systematic thinking and acting of human beings is an utterly insignificant reflection. This feeling is the guiding principle of his life and work, in so far as he succeeds in keeping himself from the shackles of selfish desire. It is beyond question closely akin to that which has possessed the religious geniuses of all ages.

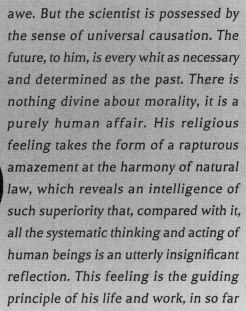

Perhaps you are a scientist (or scientific thinker) who is attracted by the fellowship and tolerant spirituality of the Craft, but worry that you might be rejected because you are not a churchgoer or a formal member of a particular religious faith. If so, here are definitions of 'supreme being" from two of the high priests of cosmological science. Both definitions are deeply moving and inspiring; either one will allow you to answer honestly and in the affirmative the question that all prospective Freemasons are asked.

Einstein: *"The harmony of natural law, which reveals an intelligence of such superiority that, compared with it, all the systematic thinking and acting of human beings is an utterly insignificant reflection."*

Newton: *"The most wise and excellent contrivance of things and final causes."*

FREEMASONRY'S QUESTION ABOUT belief in a supreme being asks Candidates to consider if their knowledge of the universe has developed to such a degree that they understand that all things are one, all things are connected, and there is a purpose to existence.

Stephen Hawking, one of the preeminent scientists of the modern era, adopts the metaphor of god (or Supreme Being) to explain his belief in the rule of order underlying the evolution of life.

[I]f we discover a complete theory, it should in time be understandable in broad principle to everyone, not just a few scientists. Then we shall all, philosophers, scientists and just ordinary people be able to take part in the discussion of the question of why it is that we and the universe exist. If we find the answer to that, it would be the ultimate triumph of human reason—for then we would know the mind of God.

In a similar vein, Albert Einstein said this about religion and science in 1930:

Common to all religions is the anthropomorphic character of their conception of God. In general, only individuals of exceptional endowments, and exceptionally high-minded communities, rise to any considerable extent above this level. But there is a third stage of religious experience which belongs to all of them, even though it is rarely found in a pure form. I call it cosmic religious feeling. The individual feels the futility of human desire and aims, and the sublimity and marvellous order which reveal themselves both in nature and the world of thought. Individual existence impresses him as *a sort of prison, and he wants to experience the universe as a single significant whole.*

And then he posed the following challenge:

How can cosmic religious feeling be communicated from one person to another, if it can give rise to no definite notion of a God and no theology? In my view, it is the most important function of art and science to awaken this feeling and keep it alive in those who are receptive to it. In this materialistic age of ours, the serious scientific workers are the only profoundly religious people.

Einstein was not a Freemason, but in these remarks he summed up one of the key intentions of the Craft—to awaken in its brethren a love and hunger for Truth.

The Philosophy of Freemasonry

By forcing prospective members to define their own beliefs, Freemasonry offers its first lesson. It encourages individuals to face up to their ideas about the purpose of the universe.

Reports of personal experience of the presence of a god are at the center of all religious faiths. Michael Persinger, a psychologist at the Laurentian University in Ontario, said the following about such direct experience of god:

Reports of meaningful and profound relationships with gods, such as Allah, Jehovah, Yahweh, or even the Great Cosmic Whole, are extraordinarily frequent. One brief episode of the God Experience can change the life of an individual. When embedded within the rules of human culture, a collection of these experiences can form the dynamic core of a religious movement.

When having a God Experience, the subject feels their ego become united with all space-time (which may be called Yahweh, Allah, God, Cosmic Consciousness, or some other idiosyncratic label, such as Great Architect of the Universe). According to Persinger, people who have these incidents typically describe them as either "spiritually mystical states" or "peak experiences."

There is a strand of Freemasonry that investigate experience at the core of so many different religions and tries to understand it. The most important Masonic writer on this subject is Walter Leslie

Wilmshurst. He wrote a book called *The Meaning of Masonry* (1922), in which he explained his ideas about this state of mind more fully. He called it "cosmic consciousness" and defined it as *"an inner vision which transcends sight as far as sight transcends touch, and a consciousness in which the contrast between the ego and the external world and the distinction between subject and object fall away."*

Freemasonry has developed a way of conveying this spiritual insight, which Einstein called "the third stage of religious experience." It does so by enabling brethren to access modes of the transcendental through myth, ritual, and symbolism. For scientists, Freemasonry provides a chance to discuss and enjoy spiritual experiences without having to compromise scientific beliefs.

Religion addresses many matters, such as birth, death, and marriage, that science and Freemasonry do not. Freemasonry has evolved to bring together individuals of any belief system to share what they have in common, but it never has had any ambitions to become a religion in its own right. Indeed it makes the point that religious belief is a matter of individual conscience for every member. It entails no doctrine of belief, and all it asks followers is that they believe in a source of order in the Universe and want to try to understand it.

The only people it excludes are atheists, as they have already decided that there is no purpose to search for. Freemasonry can offer them nothing, as it provides a forum to help its brethren join together to search for their own Truth about the meaning of life. It allows every brother to share what they have found with individuals of different religious beliefs, so that all may learn from each other.

Over the ages, the Craft has evolved and refined its ritual forms to help followers find their own answers to these big questions. It may

be that absolute Truth cannot be expressed in language and can only be revealed through a ceremony of Initiation—which is what Freemasonry offers.

Initiation

The Norwegian anthropologist and ethnographer Fredrik Barth, who studied rites of passage from boyhood to manhood in New Guinea, said that the secret knowledge of initiation is paradoxical. In many rituals, he reported, candidates are taught that the secret of the initiation is precisely that there is no secret. Alternatively, they might be told that they will not be given the secret until they reach a further stage of initiation. In these ways, the rituals promote the idea that knowledge is intrinsically ambiguous and dangerous.

This is the pattern Freemasonry follows as well. Once the Candidate is given the secrets of a Master Mason, he or she is told that they are not the "real" secrets because those have been lost and the search for the true secrets of the self must continue.

Rituals in general produce their effects in ways that may not be understood by those who carry them out. Likewise, Masonic rituals have a transcendent flavor. For brethren who take part in them, the ritual activates mysterious forces that can be sensed but not described. There is a mystical ambiguity in that they can't be performed seriously without assuming that a prescribed series of actions will have a certain result, while also feeling that these actions cannot explain the result.

But when a group of people perform rituals together it sharpens their perception that they are a troupe with clearly marked boundaries. The Tyler (the Masonic term for the Outer Guard), standing at the door of the lodge with sword in hand, marks a clear boundary between Masons and non-Masons.

IN THE END, Freemasonry, religion, and physics all deal with the same great subject—the meaning of life—and seek the same goals—an understanding of the true nature of reality. However, their approaches are markedly different. The purpose of Freemasonry is to help members know themselves and discover how they relate to society and the universe in general. In the words of W.L. Wilmshurst, *"Masonry is not non-religious, but supersectarian, and is directed to secrets and mysteries of being which popular religion does not deal with. It is ontological and philosophic, not theological."*

Science asks, "What will happen if I do this?" making no judgment regarding the morality of the action.

Religion asks, "Should I do this?" having no view on the practicality of what is to be done.

Freemasonry asks, "What can I learn about myself and my world from this?" helping individuals understand themselves.

ULTIMATELY, A SCIENTIFIC view of creation elicits a sense of profound awe and mystery, either in the vast expanse of the Universe or in the minute detail of the subatomic zoo where quarks and bosons lurk. At each end of the scale, science dissolves into deep uncertainty. For anyone trained in this perspective, it is hard to accept the idea that everything has been arranged by a personal god merely so that He might preside over humanity's struggle with good and evil. The Laws of the Great Architect must have a much wider interest than human misdeeds to have produced such a wonderful creation. If a person's ethical and moral views are based on religion, the disturbing insights of science pose enormous problems. This is where Freemasonry offers a way forward.

To become a Freemason, you must express a belief in the existence of an order at the center of creation. This is metaphorically expressed as a belief in Supreme Being, the nature of which is not questioned but left to your own conscience. Masonry leaves the individual free to believe in the immutable but statistically uncertain laws that govern the interactions of subatomic particles without ascribing human characteristics to the Great Architect of the Universe.

Here lies the truth in the statement that Freemasonry is "a peculiar system of morality." It is peculiar in the sense of being singular and unique. It teaches ethics and purpose without insisting on the need to accept any particular metaphysical concepts.

At the same time, even the physical benefits of practicing spiritual rituals are real—lower blood pressure, decreased heart rate, lower rate of respiration, reduced levels of cortisol, and a boost to the immune system. As Persinger said, spiritual practice is useful as long as religious fanaticism does not overwhelm its benefits. Freemasonry is the only spiritual system that has evolved away from the risk of religious intolerance. It teaches you how to experience oneness with creation, but it does not tell you what religious beliefs you must hold; all it asks is that you accept the idea that there is a sense of order in the universe. It is as open to the scientist as it is to the religious mystic. And it gives them both a shared symbolic system that enables them to talk about the human spirit and physical universe without offending each other's belief systems. As W.L. Wilmshurst put it,

> *Masonry is not a secular society. It is a house of the spirit. It is to be lived in the spirit as well as in the ritual. We who live it know that the sacred law of life itself, like our ceremonies that are dramatized images of that life, subjects us to repeated tests.*
> *Those who do not pass the tests remain self-inhibited from moving towards larger knowledge and deeper experience of that which is veiled at the centre of Masonic allegory.*

The symbolism and myth of Freemasonry draw on many sources—Enochian Judaism, early European craft guilds, Egyptian builders, Phoenician traders, and Norse temple builders. Its myths have been honed over thousands of years to nurture the human spirit. The purpose of Freemasonry is to help individuals learn how to live comfortably in balance with the stark reality of the cosmos. It is a heritage of ancient spiritual teaching, and it is held in trust by each generation to pass on to their sons and daughters.

There is a range of spiritual responses to be found in shared ritual. Freemasonry has many types of lodges—those that share an interest in scouting, for example, or amateur radio, or the Internet. In such shared-interest lodges, members receive the spiritual uplift of Masonic ritual and move on to discuss their hobbies in after-proceedings. Shared hobbies, however, are not enough by themselves to sustain a Mason. Members need the spiritual path that the ritual offers, no matter how they choose to follow it.

The strength and worth of a lodge rests on the quality of the communal life of its members. It depends on their united and consistent cooperation toward a common ideal. And yet, even as its success relies on the ability to form close fraternal bonds and group consciousness, Freemasonry is adapted for people who live in the real world and discharge domestic and secular duties. It is not an enclosed order; it does not call on members to follow any uniform set of rules but leaves them to live their lives in their own way. In short, Freemasonry helps members learn to harmonize their outward and inward lives, and it does so in three specific ways:

1. Emphasizing constant obedience to Moral Law.
2. Calling for "daily progress in Masonic Science" by following some form of helpful study, reflection, or meditative practice (according to personal taste and temperament).
3. Providing the symbolism of working tools and the Tracing Boards for daily contemplation and reflection.

Said Wilmshurst:

> Throughout the ages the aspirant to Initiation has found it essential to pass under the personal tuition of some expert teacher who knows the way and can give him help suited to his personal requirements. Hence the Craft, following this traditional method, declares that every new Apprentice shall find a Master and from him gain instruction.

If the members of a lodge want to grow spiritually, it is important for them to cooperate with every other Brother in an effort to realize the lodge as an organic unity of minds. Ritual should lift the spirit and refresh the individual to face the outside world. The ancient but unenforceable penalties not only link members with a more brutal past; they focus the mind on the reality of existence and warn that progress involves risk and effort. The use of rituals—which are powerful emotional tools—should not be restricted merely to satisfy the superstitious fears of people who have hostile and intolerant agendas to promote.

THOMAS JEFFERSON

Freedom of Belief

Freemasons have as much natural right to practice their spiritual ways as the members of any religion, and we should insist on that freedom of belief. Remember the words, written by American Masons, in the Declaration of Independence: "We hold these truths to be self-evident, that all men are created equal, that they are endowed by their Creator with certain unalienable Rights that among these are Life, Liberty and the pursuit of Happiness. —That to secure these rights, Governments are instituted among Men, deriving their just powers from the consent of the governed."

Freemasonry is an ancient science of the mind that can drive human ambition and achievement. It can offer great insights that do not conflict with modern science.

THE PATH OF FREEMASONRY IS A WAY INTO THE MYSTERY OF THE INNER SELF- WHETHER YOU CALL IT SOUL, SPIRIT, OR STATE OF CONSCIOUSNESS.

It is useful to remember that since the time of Henry VIII the monarchs of England have always been head of the Church of England (except for a brief period during the English Civil War when England became a republic and the Archbishop of Canterbury took

over the role). As temporal and spiritual leaders, many of the kings have also been Freemasons, beginning with James I (James VI of Scotland and sponsor of the English translation of the bible known the King James Bible), who brought Freemasonry down to England from Scotland to succeed Queen Elizabeth I on the throne in 1603. This was the moment at which the crowns of Scotland and England came together, though it was some time before the two parliaments were combined.

As recently as 1952, both King George VI, head of the Church of England and Defender of the Faith, and the Archbishop of Canterbury, Geoffrey Fisher, were Senior Freemasons in the United Grand Lodge of England. Both of those men found, as do many other brethren, that Freemasonry is a philosophy that seeks to learn from all faiths about the nature of Truth, and is not in any way a religion itself. It supports religion and remains stalwartly tolerant and protective of each individual Mason's beliefs.

It provides a forum and a shared neutral language to discuss what all seekers after Truth share. And it has created ways to avoid the conflict that can arise from the discussion of religion and politics. Translated into familiar terms, the philosophy of Freemasonry is to help members recognize the transcendental condition of consciousness that exists within each person, but does not seek to impose any particular religious doctrine about what Masons call "the knowledge of the Center."

James I was the first king after Henry VII, more than a century earlier, to serve as head of the Church of England while holding the right to attend the General Assembly of the Presbyterian Church. He was also a Scotsman and a Freemason. The next thing we will look at, therefore, is the early Scottish history of Freemasonry.

SCOTTISH ROOTS

IN A SMALL MASONIC HALL in a little city on the banks of the River Tey in Scotland hangs a painting of an important event in Masonic history—the initiation of King James VI of Scotland in 1601. The painting belongs to the Lodge of Scoon and Perth, in the city of Perth. If you look at the entry for this lodge on the Roll of the Grand Lodge of Scotland, it says simply that the lodge existed before 1658 but has no previous written records.

In 1658, the brethren of the lodge decided to write out a set of rules that explained how it was to be run. The document is called the Lodge

LODGE OF SCOON AND PERTH, TODAY

Charter. It is signed by the Right Worshipful Master, J Roch, and his two wardens, Mr. Measone and Mr. Norie. Their charter is the first written record of the event depicted in the painting hanging on the wall of the lodge room. It reads as follows:

> *In the reign of his Majesty King James the sixth, of blessed Memory, who, by the said John Mylne was by the king's own desire entered Freeman, Mason and Fellow-Craft. During his lifetime he maintained the same as any member of the Lodge of Scoon, so that this lodge is the most famous lodge within the kingdom.*

The name John Mylne was important in the early history of Freemasonry, as three generations of men with the same name held the Mastership of the Lodge of Scoon and Perth between the late 1500s and 1658. In the latter year, James Roch became the master. This is the Bro. "J Roch" who signed the charter that told of the initiation of James VI as a Freemason in 1601.

Fifteen years after that, John, the son of the "said John Mylne" who initiated King James, carved a statue of the king in Edinburgh. In 1631, John was appointed Master Mason to King James's son and heir, Charles I; in 1636, John passed the title on to his eldest son, also named John Mylne. This third-generation John Mylne had become a member of the Lodge of Edinburgh by 1633. Later, in 1641, he took part in a Masonic meeting in Newcastle where Sir Robert Moray became the first Mason known to have been initiated on English soil.

The two most famous early Freemasons, King James VI of Scotland and Sir Robert Moray, both were initiated by the Mylne family.

Perhaps Bro. John Mylne told Bro. Sir Robert Moray how his grand-father had initiated James VI. After the English Civil War, with a number of other Freemasons, Moray went on to found the Royal Society, which became one of the most important scientific societies in the world.

The answer is political, and it involves a man named William Schaw, who on December 21, 1583, became Master of Works to King James. This position put him in charge of construction and maintenance of all royal property.

William Schaw and the Schaw Statutes

Schaw clearly had diplomatic as well as building skills, as he helped entertain Danish ambassadors trying to negotiate the return of Orkney and Shetland islands to Denmark. Schaw got on well with the Danes, and James sent him to Denmark in 1589 to escort his new bride, Anne of Denmark, to Scotland. Schaw went on to be Queen Anne's

SCHAW MONUMENT

Chamberlain and her favorite courtier. His monument in Dunfermline Cathedral reads as follows:

Queen Anne ordered a monument to be set up to the memory of a most admirable and most upright man lest the recollection of his high character, which deserves to be honoured for all time, should fade as his body crumbles into dust.

Schaw took an active interest in Masons and their lodges from 1590 onwards. He decided to organize the Mason Craft under a number of regional wardens, so that he could make sure they paid all their taxes and fees. He also appointed a Grand Warden for the Freemasons of Aberdeen, Banff, and Kincarne, as recorded in a letter written under the authority of the king's Privy Seal to Patrick Copland of Udoch (near Aberdeen). Copland was the first Grand Warden to be appointed.

Eight years later, Schaw decided to ask the king to appoint him to a new position, General Warden of the Freemasons of Scotland. To ensure that he would be accepted by the secretive Freemasons, Schaw called a meeting of Master Masons of Edinburgh, held on the Feast of St. John the Evangelist in 1598. At the meeting, the Master Masons approved his appointment and issued a document known as the **First Schaw Statute.**

As the king's Master of Works, Schaw was already the commissioning agent for the throne in respect of all state building works. By becoming General Warden of Masons, he set out to rationalize that

state of affairs. The First Schaw Statute contained 22 clauses. The first of
them required that all Masons

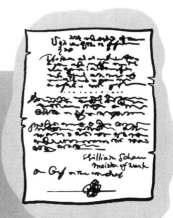

observe and keep all the good
ordinances set down before,
concerning the privileges of
their Craft set down by their
predecessors of good memory
and that they be true to one
another and live charitably
together as becomes sworn
brethren and companions of the Craft.

Every new Master must accept all of these Charges before being allowed to take control of a lodge.

The rest of the 22 clauses dictate how the lodges should be governed and how the work of the masons should be managed. Two are particularly interesting. One of them is the first health and safety directive ever issued to the building trade:

All Masters, in charge of works, be careful to see their scaffolds and ladders are surely set and placed, to the effect that through their negligence and sloth no hurt or harm come unto any persons that works at the said work, under pain of discharging of them hereafter from working as Masters having charge of any work, but they shall be subject all the rest of their days to work under or with another principal Master having charge of the work.

This was stern discipline for any Master Mason who did not take care that his workers were properly secured when toiling in the heights of a great cathedral or a Scottish grand house. Factory inspectors today would not quarrel with the intentions and sanctions of this 16th century Masonic legislation.

The other interesting item describes how the Master of a Lodge should be chosen:

A Master will be elected each year to have the charge over every lodge so that the General Warden can send instruction to that elected Master as he needs to.

Here was a highly democratic system in operation a full half-century before the English Civil War addressed the same questions of democratic accountability to the king of England.

It took account of the ancient traditions of the order and respected their rituals, while making proper provision for safe working conditions and regular democratic feedback from the Masters of the Lodges. The statutes were endorsed by all the Master Masons who attended the Feast of St. John meeting in Edinburgh in 1598, as recorded in their closing statement:

> *And for fulfilling and observing of these ordinances, set down as said here, the group of Master Masons here assembled this day binds and obliges themselves hereto to be faithful. And therefore has requested the said General Warden to sign them with his own hand, to the effect that an authentic copy hereof may be sent to every lodge within this realm.*

The First Schaw Statute began an important Masonic tradition that has carried through to the present day. It called on all lodges to keep written records of their meetings, referred to as Minutes. Before a lodge can do any business, it must read and approve the Minutes of its previous meeting. The oldest known lodge Minutes today are those of Edinburgh St. Mary's Chapel, which started to keep Minute books immediately after the 1598 meeting with Schaw.

The First Schaw Statute also tells us a lot about early Freemasonry. From it we know that Scottish brethren met in lodges; that these lodges were ruled by Masters and Wardens (one Master with a Senior Warden and a Junior Warden to support him); that there was a system of meetings at a higher level than the lodge; that lodges were obliged to keep written records of their activities; and that they were honor-bound to observe the ancient traditions of their Craft.

As all of these practices are still followed in modern

Freemasonry, Schaw is credited with formalizing the present-day system of Masonic lodges. A lodge is not just the building where Masons meet; it is also the body of individuals who make up that group. It has its own traditions, hierarchy, and records to prove what it has decided. And it is a democratically run unit inherited from a time when democracy was all but unknown in Europe.

Indeed there was a long-established lodge on the west coast of Scotland that had not been consulted. Known today as Mother Kilwinning, this lodge was located on the coast of Ayr, on the grounds of Kilwinning Abbey. The Estate of Kilwinning had once formed part of the lands of the Sinclair family, and some of the Masons dispersed from Roslin in the 15th century seem to have established themselves in this small seaside town. For some years previously, the Masters of

Mother Kilwinning lodge had been issuing charters to other groups of masons to form themselves into new lodges, and claimed rights over the Mason Craft in Ayrshire.

Schaw's First Statute did not recognize Kilwinning in the new Masonic ranking. The Masons of Kilwinning threatened to oppose it, and Schaw had to do something to maintain his authority. When, as General Warden of the Craft, he called another meeting on the next Feast Day of St. John the Evangelist, Mother Kilwinning Lodge sent Bro. Archibald Barclay as their spokesman. Barclay insisted that they should have a role in the new way of ruling the Craft, and Schaw decided to make a deal with them.

In 1599, on the Feast of St. John, Schaw issued a Second Statute from Holyrood House. The new document confirmed the statements in the First Statute but accorded formal status to Kilwinning Lodge. Schaw confirmed that Kilwinning could maintain its practice of electing officers on the eve of the winter solstice. It was assigned the rank *of Second Lodge of Scotland,* and its Master and Wardens would have the right to be present at the election of all other Wardens of Lodges in Lanarkshire, Glasgow, Ayr, and Carrick. The Master of Kilwinning would have the power to summon and judge all Masters of lodges within this area. This authority was delegated by Schaw himself, now confirmed as the all-powerful General Warden of the Craft. Finally, the Master and Wardens of Kilwinning were to conduct regular tests of Masons within their jurisdiction to ensure that they were properly trained in what was called *"the art and craft of science and of the antient art of memory."*

Thus, Schaw had settled Freemasonry with a stable structure. But he had even greater ambitions for the new organization. He wanted the king to become Grand Master of the Order, and he wanted a Royal Charter conferring this status on the Craft forever. There was one problem. The Masons would not accept a non-Mason, or what they called a *cowan*, as their Grand Master. If Schaw was to make King James the Grand Master Mason, he would first have to make the king a Mason.

In 1584, meanwhile, William Schaw had helped his close friend Alexander Seton (later Earl of Dunfermline, a member of Aberdeen Lodge) to design a house for Lord Somerville. The master mason Seton had employed to carry out the work was none other than John Mylne, who in 1601 was Master of the Lodge of Scoon and Perth. Seton's lodge was located in the village of Scoon (modern spelling Scone), the ancient coronation site for the kings of Scotland. Scottish monarchs have traditionally been crowned at Moot Hill, in the grounds of Scone Palace. Schaw thus decided that this was an appropriate Lodge to initiate the king into Freemasonry. John Mylne was happy to cooperate.

Once the king was an accepted Mason, Schaw had everything in place to install a Royal Grand Master Mason for the Craft. Once that was done, a Royal Charter could be issued to confirm his own authority as Lord General Warden of the Craft. James VI, who loved rituals, amateur dramatics, and dressing up, from all accounts delighted in the ceremony that initiated him into the ancient mysteries of the Mason Word.

But the Masons of Scotland did not want Schaw to take total control of their order—and they had an idea to prevent it. They claimed they already had a Grand Master, William Sinclair, Laird of Roslin (a direct descendant of the man who had commissioned Rosslyn Chapel in 1440).

William the Wastrel

William Schaw had seemed on the verge of obtaining Royal sanction to control the Craft and to take his share of its ability to earn. He also had the support of Mother Kilwinning Lodge for his second statutes. But trying to use John Mylne and the Lodge of Scoon and Perth to foist the king onto the Craft as a Royal Grand Master was going a step too far.

When he allowed Kilwinning to act as a minor Grand Lodge, the other lodges realized that Schaw could be forced to adjust his ideas. Getting the Lodge of Scoon and Perth to initiate James VI was Schaw's first move toward uniting the Lodges of Scotland under the

Grand Mastership of the king. But the consequence of adopting the Lodge of Scoon and Perth as his mother Lodge would to make, as the minutes of the lodge say, *"this lodge the most famous lodge within the kingdom."* This would have undermined all the jockeying for position that had gone on earlier. Edinburgh had been established as first lodge, Kilwinning was officially number two, and the Lodge of Stirling was third in seniority. If the Lodge of Scoon and Perth were to become the Royal Grand Master's Lodge, it would automatically take precedence over all the others. Thus, by initiating the king, the Lodge of Scoon and Perth was poised to outflank all the others. John Mylne, the Right Worshipful Master, had positioned himself to become William Schaw's second in command.

The lodges in the east of Scotland—Edinburgh, St. Andrews, Haddington, Acheson Haven, and Dunfermline—were not happy at this prospect and put pressure on Schaw to acknowledge another supposed ancient authority in Freemasonry, William St Clair, Baron of Roslin.

William St Clair, the third and last St Clair Earl of Orkney, the builder of Rosslyn Chapel, and the figure whom the Masons claimed as their hereditary patron, was long dead. His estates had been forcibly split up after his failed coup in the 15th century. The Barony of Roslin had been transferred to his baby son Oliver, via him to another William, and then to an Edward before vesting in the particular William Sinclair who figures in this story.

This William followed the Roman Catholic faith, a fact that did not endear him to the Presbyterian Kirk (Church) of Scotland. Even though Rosslyn Chapel was not registered as a Parish Kirk, William had his child baptized there. He bribed a local minister to hold the service, but this backfired when the cleric was coerced into making a public apology by the Elders of the Parish of Dalkeith. The Elders accused William of "keeping images and other monuments of idolatry in Roslin." They tried to question him about the offense, but he had already been jailed for making threats to the king.

The officials were waiting when William was freed from prison. They insisted that Roslin Chapel was not authorized as a place of Presbyterian worship, though William's tenants were holding services there. He was told to force his tenants to attend the official Parish Church and set a good example by becoming an Elder himself. William declined to take the office, on grounds that he was "insufficient" for it. This was

a fair self-assessment, as soon afterwards he was caught "in flagrante" with a local barmaid. William made the situation worse by insisting that he could not recall if all the bastards he had sired were baptized. The outraged Elders sentenced him to serve public penance on the repentance stool (an elevated seat in the Parish Kirk used for ritual humiliation). William declined to cooperate unless he was given a couple of pints of good wine to help pass the time.

To keep the peace and restrain him from attacking people, local magistrates frequently had William bound over. In addition to fighting, he was known for womanizing—court records describe him as "a lewd man, who kept a miller's daughter for the purpose of fornication." He eventually left his wife and his son (also William) and ran away to Ireland with a mistress.

This was the man the Masons of east Scotland preferred as their Patron, rather than have John Mylne and the Lodge of Scoon and Perth take precedence over them. The Laird of Roslin, whom they claimed as their hereditary Grand Master, was known locally as William the Wastrel. To prefer this reprobate to King James as their leader shows just how far the older lodges were prepared to go to thwart the ambitions of Mylne and his lodge. The only way to foil the intentions of the Mylne family that Schaw had unleashed was to appeal to the opening sentence of the First Schaw Statute:

> that they observe and keep all the good ordinances set down before concerning the privileges of their Craft by their predecessors of good memory

The First St Clair Charter follows this line with the following:

> Be it known to all men that the Deacons, Masters and Freeman of the Masons with the realm of Scotland with the express consent and assent of William Schaw, Master of Work to our Sovereign Lord do assert that from age to age it has been observed amongst us that the Lairds of Roslin have ever been Patrons and Protectors of use and

our privileges like as our predecessors has obeyed and acknowledged them as Patrons and Protectors.

In the end, Schaw failed to get a Royal Charter to run the Freemasons because the older lodges insisted on sticking to a tradition linked to the Sinclairs of Roslin. The outrageous character of the man to whom they gave their allegiance suggests that the tradition must have been well known to them. If they had not felt it would be accepted by all Masons, they would have had to go along with Schaw's plan and take His Majesty King James VI as their new Royal Patron. The fact that the king joined the Craft did encourage many of his courtiers to do so as well. Among them were Lord Alexander, Lord Hamilton, and David Ramsay (Clockmaker to the king and gentleman of the Privy Chamber), all of whom joined the Lodge of Edinburgh.

I LIKE THIS OUTFIT TOO

Schaw's death in 1602 and King James's removal to London to take up the crown of England, Ireland, and Wales, left Freemasonry in Scotland in a state of confusion. King James loved to take part in rituals where he could act out the role of King Solomon. (The Master of a Lodge traditionally takes on this role during the opening and closing ceremonies.) James was not secretive about it. Sir John Harrington, who spent an evening at James VI's court while entertaining King Christian of Denmark in 1617, reported:

After dinner the ladies and gentlemen of the Court enacted the Queen of Sheba coming to King Solomon's Temple. The lady who took the part of the Queen of Sheba was, however, too drunk to keep her balance on

> *the steps and fell over onto King Christian's lap, covering him with wine, cream, jelly, beverages, cakes, spices and other good matters which she was carrying in her hands.*

James became so obsessed with reenacting the events surrounding Solomon's Temple that his courtiers began to call him the British Solomon. He also carried out regular Freemasonic ceremonies. William Preston, in his book *Illustrations of Freemasonry* (1772) reports:

> In 1607, the foundation stone of the Palace of Whitehall was laid by King James, and his wardens who were attended by many brothers, clothed in form. The ceremony was conducted with the greatest pomp and splendor.

THUS, THROUGH MASTER OF WORKS WILLIAM SCHAW, KING JAMES VI DEVELOPED THE MODERN LODGE SYSTEM OF FREEMASONRY IN SCOTLAND PRIOR TO COMING TO ENGLAND.

He made Speculative Freemasonry fashionable at the Scottish Court and then brought the rituals of Masonry to England.

The first account we have of a Freemason being initiated on English soil is about another Scot, a soldier in the rebellious Covenanter's Army that marched against King Charles I of England during the English Civil War. He was initiated into the Lodge of Edinburgh by military members of that lodge stationed in Newcastle.

Sir Robert Moray

The first Freemason initiated outside Scotland for whom we have a written record is Robert Moray. He was born on March 10, 1609, and educated in mathematics and civil engineering at St. Andrews University before joining the "Scots Guard" of Louis XIII, king of France, in 1633. Moray became a favorite of Cardinal Richelieu, Louis's Minster for Foreign Affairs and the political power behind the French throne. Richelieu recruited Moray as a spy, which was how he came to be in Newcastle with the Covenanters in 1638, working for the French.

That year, the Scots rebelled against Charles I because he had tried to undermine the Presbyterian Kirk and replace it with the Church of England. Richelieu, a Roman Catholic, promoted Moray to Lieutenant-Colonel in Louis's elite Scots Guard and sent him to Scotland to help the rebels there make trouble for Charles and the Church of England. Moray, an expert in military fortifications and logistics, became quartermaster-general for the rebel Army. As such, he was in charge of laying out the Army's camps and defenses, for which his knowledge of mathematics and surveying proved extremely useful. Moray marched south toward the Tyne with the Scottish Army and played his part in defeating the Earl of Stafford at the Battle of Newcastle. Moray was initiated into the Lodge of Edinburgh when the Scots held that city, by Bro. John Mylne. The latter was the grandson of the John Mylne, who had initiated King James. Mylne was assisted in the ceremony by Bro. General Hamilton of the Covenanters.

The Scots forced King Charles to accept the rule of the Kirk in Scotland. As part of the deal, they tried to get Charles to pay the back wages of their army in Newcastle. Richelieu was pleased with the outcome but died before the deal could be completed in 1642. As soon as Moray heard the news, he dumped the Scots rebels and rode south to Oxford to tell Charles about Richelieu's demise. He offered to act as a go-between with King Louis of France, who was Charles's father in law. With Richelieu dead, Moray knew that the French King could easily change his attitude to Charles. Charles took up Moray's offer and knighted him, granting him the rank to act as his envoy.

On January 10, 1643, Sir Robert became a mediator between King Charles I, the Scots, and the French. In doing so, he became a trusted friend of both kings. Louis promoted him to full colonel in the Scots Guard as a reward for his help. Unluckily for Robert, however, Louis died on May 14, 1643, and was succeeded by his son, the four-year-old Louis XIV. Queen Anne, Louis XIII's widow, became Regent and relied completely on Cardinal Mazarin. He disliked both the English king and Robert Moray, which was not good for either one.

On November 24, 1643, Moray was captured by the Duke of Bavaria and thrown into prison. He was eventually offered for ransom to the

French, but Mazarin refused and left him to rot. On April 28, 1645, Mazarin changed his mind and paid £16,500 (a few million dollars in today's money) for Moray's release and had him sent to London. Why the change of mind?

Charles I had been defeated by Oliver Cromwell's troops at the Battle of Naseby, the decisive campaign in the Civil War, and was forced to negotiate with both the Scots, who still held much of northern England, and the English Parliament. Mazarin sent Moray as a member of the French ambassadorial party to support the Scottish commissioners, among them General Hamilton. Hamilton, who had initiated Morey, was appointed by the Scots Parliament to negotiate with the king. Mazarin realized that Morey had influence with the Scots, so he ransomed him to take part in the drawn-out and awkward talks between the defeated king and his victorious people in the hope of promoting the interests of France.

The dialogue broke down, however, and Moray persuaded Charles to flee to Newark, where he gave himself up to General Hamilton of the Scots Army. The Scots took Charles to Newcastle and, on December 24, 1646, Moray set up a chance for him to flee to exile in France. To make the escape possible, Sir Robert got a lady's dress for the king to don as disguise. The plan was for Charles to slip away to a ship that Moray had ready to sail from Tynemouth. But the king was afraid of being shamed should he be arrested in women's clothing and refused to go along with the plan.

The history of the English Civil War might have been changed if Moray had managed to get Charles to France. More than likely, Britain would have remained a republic instead of becoming a constitutional monarchy. Instead, the Scots sold Charles to Cromwell, and the latter agreed to pay the Army's back wages. Charles returned to London, went on trial for treason, and was executed by beheading. Moray sailed for France and exile.

After Charles's death on January 30, 1649, the Earl of Lauderdale, a Mason from the Lodge of Edinburgh, asked fellow Mason Moray to try to persuade the Prince of Wales to go to Scotland to be crowned Charles II, King of Scots. The coronation took place at Scoon in 1650, after which Charles II led a Scots army south to recover England from Cromwell. He was defeated at the Battle of Dunbar, however, and, after famously hiding up an oak tree, fled to France. Moray remained in Scotland.

Shortly after Charles's flight, Moray married Sophia Lindsey, the beautiful sister of the Earl of Balcarres. In July 1652, the couple returned to Edinburgh for the birth of their first child, and Moray plotted to raise a new Scots army to restore Charles to the English throne. Neither the child nor the army were to be. Sophia died in childbirth on January 2, 1653, with the baby stillborn, and Cromwell defeated the Scots army at the Battle of Loch Garry soon after.

Moray was then accused by his rivals of betraying the king and sent to prison. He wrote directly to Charles to plead his innocence. The king believed him, and Moray went to join him in exile in France.

Back in Paris by 1655, Moray resigned his commission in the Scots Guard and retired to Maastricht in Holland. In September 1659, a year after Oliver Cromwell's death, Moray was called back to Paris

to take part in negotiations with George Monck, Duke of Albermarle, to have Charles restored to the throne of England.

Upon Charles's return to England as king in late June 1660, Moray went back to Maastricht to spy on the Dutch, who were threatening war with England. When he finally went to London, Charles granted him a "grace-and-favour house" within the grounds of the Palace of Whitehall. From there, Moray used his Masonic connections to bring together the two sides of the Civil War and founded a sort of scientific think tank to solve the technical problems of the Royal Navy. The organization was chartered in 1662 as the Royal Society.

One of the many Freemasons that Moray recruited for this scientific venture was the first Englishman known to be initiated into an English lodge, in 1646. That man was the famous diarist Elias Ashmole.

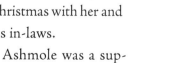

Elias Ashmole

Ashmole was born in Lichfield, Staffordshire, on May 23, 1617. He grew up to be both a solicitor and an astrologer. He is perhaps best known for the Ashmolean Museum he set up at Oxford University.

At the age of 16, he left Lichfield to move to London and lived there with his mother's cousin, Baron Pagit. It was at this time that he began to keep a diary. By 1638, in his early twenties, he had qualified as a solicitor and married Eleanor Manwaring, a young lady from Smallwood, near Warrington, whom he had met at Pagit's house. Eleanor became pregnant in 1641 and went to Smallwood to stay with her parents for the birth. Sadly, she and the baby died in childbirth in early December. Elias did not learn of her death until travelling to Cheshire to spend Christmas with her and his in-laws.

Ashmole was a supporter of Charles I, but 1641 was not a good year to be a Royalist in London. The King and Parliament were quarrelling more often, and civil war was looming. In May 1643, Ashmole finally was forced out of London and moved to Oxford, where Charles I had set up his court. At Brasenose College, he studied natural philosophy, mathematics, astronomy, and astrology, though it is unclear if he was officially enrolled. There is no record of his graduating. Apparently he was living at the college as what is called a "stranger," sponsored by his uncle by marriage, Sir Henry Manwaring.

In March 1645, Ashmole met Captain Wharton, a senior officer in the king's garrison of Oxford, who shared his interest in astrology. The two men got along well, and within a month Wharton appointed him one of four Masters of Ordnance for the city. When King Charles returned to Oxford after his defeat at Naseby, Ashmole was set to work to defend the city against Parliamentary attack. When the king left to try to make a deal with Scots at Newark, Ashmole went to Worcester to become the King's Commissioner of Excise.

Two days before Christmas in 1645, Ashmole arrived at Worcester and was sworn in as its Commissioner. He lost no time in ingratiating himself with the local bigwigs, dining with Lords Brereton and Astley, and presenting his letter of reference. He wrote in his

diary that he also met Sir Gilbert Gerard, the Royalist Governor of Worcester. Clearly, Ashmole was on the side of the king and made no secret of his loyalty.

That January, Ashmole helped Lord Astley prepare his forces to relieve Chester. He cast horoscopes repeatedly to predict the course of the war and interpreted his dreams to foretell the future. In April 1646, he wrote that he dreamed "The King went from Oxford in disguise to the Scots." This is one of the few accurate predictions that Ashmole made, as Charles did leave Oxford and surrender to the Scots at Newark.

Oxford fell on June 20, 1846, Lichfield fell on July 14, 1646, and Captain Ashmole was among those who surrendered ten days later. The fall of Worcester signaled the end of Charles I's hopes. As a Royalist officer, Ashmole was forbidden to live within the city limits of London and couldn't practice law. Having thrown in his lot with King Charles, he was out of political favor and out of a job. Casting horoscopes for signs of a change in luck, he imagined a return to London and the chance to marry a wealthy widow.

Any wealthy widow would do. Mrs. Cole, Mrs. Minshull, Mrs. Ireland, Lady Thornborough, Mrs. March, Lady Fitton, and Lady Manwaring all figured in the erotic and mercenary dreams that the 29-year-old confided to his diary during this period

He never did persuade a wealthy widow to marry him and had to find another way of making a living. The Articles of Surrender he had signed forced him either to return to his home or to go overseas and never again bear arms against the Parliament of England or do anything wilfully to prejudice its affairs. With no family home to return to, his only living family member was his father-in-law, Peter Manwaring of Smallwood. So Ashmole returned to Cheshire to live with the father of his deceased wife.

For a while, he scratched out a living by carrying out simple legal duties for his father-in-law. But he was highly stressed and feeling sorry for himself. "This night I first perceived a boil to rise upon my

arse," he confided to his diary. His joints were aching, and he was constipated. He began to record the number of stools he passed each day and cast horoscopes to find out if he should "get a fortune by a wife without pains and easily."

What rich widow would want a constipated outcast with an enormous boil on his backside is a question he avoided asking his stars.

Yet Ashmole was ambitious and finally hit on an idea for succeeding in life.

On October 17, 1646, he borrowed money from his cousin, Col. Henry Manwaring, and bought a horse from Congleton Horse Fair. By October 25, he was on his way to London despite the pledge he had made not to live in the capital. For some reason, he felt that he would be allowed to ignore the restraining order he had signed at the surrender of the Worcester.

On the November 20, 1646, Ashmole set up home in London and began to mix with astrologers, alchemists, and mathematicians Among them was William Lilly, the author of a much-respected university textbook on *Christian Astrology*. What had happened to change Ashmole's fortunes and make him acceptable to such a respected and successful supporter of Parliament?

WILLIAM LILLY

The answer is that he had become a Freemason. His cousin, Col. Henry Manwaring, had proposed him as a member of a lodge that met in Warrington. It still exists today and is known as the Lodge of Lights. Ashmole was initiated into Freemasonry on the afternoon of October 16, 1646. His membership of the Craft was key to meeting influential people and allowing him to move to London. A note in the papers of the Public Record Office confirms the unlawful nature of his move to London. "Ashmole doth make his abode in London notwithstanding the Act of Parliament to the contrary," it reads.

He had changed virtually overnight, transformed from a despairing outcast suffering from constipation, aching joints, repeated failures in love, and boils on his bum, to an enthusiastic and bold adventurer. He was accepted in London society. The only change in his status was his membership in the Freemasons. His diary entry for October 16, 1646, reads as follows:

4H.30 P.M. I was made a free Mason at Warrington in Lancashire, with Coll: Henry Manwaring of Karincham in Cheshire. The names of those that were then of the Lodge, Mr: Rich Penket Warden, Mr: James Collier, Mr: Rich: Sankey, Henry Littler, John Ellam, Rich: Ellam & Hugh Brewer.

The men making up this lodge were mainly local landowners, and all would have been well known to the Manwaring family. One notable fact about the membership is that it was drawn from both sides of the Civil War, including a Roundhead Colonel and two Royalist Captains.

Ashmole was revitalized by joining the Craft. He stopped drifting and found work. His astrological inquiries, as recorded in his diary, show that he had been afraid of moving to London before his initiation. After joining the lodge, he was transformed.

His new circle of Masonic friends revolved around William Oughtred, a mathematician, an alchemist, an astrologer, and the

inventor of the slide rule. Through Oughtred, he met such other notables as Seth Ward, Jonas Moore, Thomas Henshaw, Christopher Wren, William Lilly, George Wharton, Thomas Wharton, and Edward Gunter. He became a regular visitor to Gresham College, the regular meeting place of the founding members of the Royal Society. By June 17, 1652, Ashmole was so well established in London that he had a visit from the Reverend John Wilkins, Oliver Cromwell's brother-in-law, who brought with him Christopher Wren, later the architect of St. Paul's Cathedral. Wilkins was a successful Parliamentarian academic and the Warden of Wadham College, Oxford, where Wren had been his student.

Ashmole wrote in his dairy, "Doctor Wilkins & Mr: Wren came to visit me at Blackfriars. This was the first time I saw the Doctor." Wren had just been appointed a fellow of All Souls, Cambridge. Both visitors were close to Cromwell and highly successful, but—now that he was a Mason—they were happy to visit a disgraced Royalist ex-officer living illegally in London.

In June 1647, William Lilly asked Ashmole to create a new index for his text book *Christian Astrology,* a prestigious text used widely in universities. Ashmole cast a horoscope for the best time to start the work and fixed on ten minutes after twelve noon on the fifth day of the month. If only metaphorically, the stars were smiling on him—his association with Lilly greatly increased his status in the Masonic society of London

Ashmole's *Diary* is a series of jottings about his business, military, and romantic affairs rather than a complete daily record of what he did. He writes about his attempts to marry and quotes a number of Masonic dedications, yet only twice does he mention going to Masonic meetings. He began to write a complete *History of Freemasonry*, in which he may have written more about his attitude to the Craft, but sadly this work has been lost.

Ashmole was not afraid to promote his new status as a Mason, using Masonic symbols in the front of his books and publicly accepting Masonic dedications and tributes. He saw Freemasonry as a means to an end. Much as he had cold bloodedly set out to marry a rich widow, so he set out to join a Society that would protect him if he returned to London and that could provide him with a ready-made circle of useful contacts. So if Elias Ashmole is not the best advertisement for Freemasonry, his association with the Order did improve his character. He became a strong supporter of the new Royal Society and endowed Oxford University with the cabinet of curiosities that became the world-renowned Ashmolean Museum.

As the 17th century drew to a close, the constitutional monarchy established by Charles II was threatened by the behavior of his successor, James II. Attempting to return to the bad old days of despotic rule, James was forced into exile by the Glorious Revolution in December 1688 and eventually replaced by a new line of constitutional monarchs from the Electorate of Hanover. This process, as we are about to see, threw the Stuart-inspired system of Masonic lodges into turmoil.

THE FIRST GRAND LODGES

I N THE EARLY YEARS OF FREEMASONRY, as we have seen, the original Lodge of Aberdeen trained Master Masons in both stoneworking and the use of symbols. Once they had been tested—or, as Masons say, "proved"—they would be given the Mason Word, freed from their Apprenticeship, and made a Fellow of the Craft, or what Masons call a Fellowcraft. Many of these Craftsmen moved away to get work and joined other local incorporations of Masons. In time they formed their own lodges, each developing their own interpretation of the basic lessons and passed on the symbolic teachings

they had found so inspiring. In this way, Freemasonry spread southward through Scotland and eventually into England, where it took root in York. Before William Schaw, there was no organization in control of Freemasonry. Any group of seven or more brethren who knew the secrets of symbolism, ritual, and the Mason Word could form a lodge and initiate new Masons.

As of 1599, the Freemasons had only two ceremonies— a ceremony of Initiation to welcome an Apprentice, and a ceremony for becoming a Craftsman at the end of the Apprenticeship. Later, a third ceremony would be introduced to make a Fellowcraft a Master or Warden of the Lodge. The Schaw Statutes brought the modern lodge system into being, and additional degrees came along as lodge rituals became more formalized.

By the early 17th century, Freemasonry was widely established in Scotland and had become known for its secret knowledge of "the Mason Word," "Mystic Symbols," and the "Art of Memory." Each lodge was independent, having only to follow the broad rules laid down by a General Warden appointed by the Crown.

The operative builders under the guidance of Masters Alexander Stuart, David Menzies, and Matthew Wright had been interested in the art of construction. They were, after all, employed to extend St. Nicholas's Kirk in Aberdeen. But they were also interested in the spiritual power of the symbols they carved into public buildings. The lodge in Aberdeen began to teach its knowledge of symbols to men who were not working stonemasons. This outreach began under the mastership of Alexander Stuart, who was also an alderman on the Aberdeen Burgh Council. Before this time, working stonemasons had simply formed corporations to protect the interests of the craftsmen. In Aberdeen, the lodge began to share its teachings about symbols with worthy men of other professions. The fact that a Mason of the Lodge of Aberdeen became an Alderman of the Burgh (rather than just an employee of the Council) shows how the practice of intermingling patrons and craftsmen began early in the history of Freemasonry. By the 17th century, The Mark Book (a volume kept by the lodge that recorded the names and identification marks of Masons

accepted as Fellowcrafts) shows that the Lodge of Aberdeen was regularly taking in important citizens of Aberdeen who were not working on the fabric of the Kirk.

As we saw in the previous chapter, the Stuart kings organized Freemasonry into a formal system, with rules and ways of reporting to a higher authority than the lodge. But they created what today we would call a "flat management structure." There were no layers of middle management between the Master of a Lodge, elected by the brethren, and the General Warden, appointed by the king. This basic structure lasted for about the first 100 years of Freemasonry, but, as the movement spread south into England, more complicated systems developed.

YORK MINSTER

The Grand Lodge of York

The earliest attempt to form an organization to create and control new lodges and to run English Freemasonry took place in York. Itinerant stonemasons who had trained in one or another of the early Scottish lodges were working on the Gothic cathedral of York Minster. In the 16th century, they formed a lodge known as St. George's Chapel, which in turn gave birth to a scattering of daughter lodges in the northern English county of Yorkshire. In 1705, several of these lodges came together to meet as a Grand Lodge of York, under the direction of Sir George Tempest, whom they elected as their Grand Master. Sir George was succeeded by the Rt. Hon. Robert Benson, Lord Mayor of York. During Benson's reign, the fraternity held a number of meetings to celebrate the feast of St. John. Sir William Robinson succeeded Benson, and Freemasonry in the north increased considerably under his guidance. Robinson was succeeded by Sir Walter Hawkesworth, and when his term ended, Sir George

Tempest was elected Grand Master for a second time. Charles Fairfax became Grand Master in 1714, and the Grand Lodge assembled regularly. During this period, Sir Walter Hawkesworth, Edward Bell, Charles Bathurst, Edward Thomson, John Johnson, and John Marsden filled the office of Grand Master in York.

York Freemasonry drew its authority from the early lodge established at York Minster, which dated back almost to the beginning of Freemasonry. Because it was never associated with the patronage of the Stuart kings, it was not subject to the political problems that dogged the formation of a Grand Lodge in London (discussed later in this chapter).

The two Grand Lodges existed for many years, and many new lodges flourished in both parts of the kingdom under their separate jurisdictions. The Grand Lodge in London, encouraged by King James and the nobility, acquired influence and reputation. The Grand Lodge in York attracted fewer members of the nobility and gradually began to decline.

The Grand Lodge in the south went by the name of the Grand Lodge of England, but the authority of the Grand Lodge in York held sway and went unchallenged. Indeed it was said that every Mason in the kingdom held it in the highest veneration and considered himself bound by the Antient Charges, which were first published in England by that assembly.

To be ranked as descendants of the original York masons has become the glory and boast of the brethren in almost every country where York Rite Masonry is established. For it was in York that English Masonry was first established by the charter of a Grand Lodge.

A few Brethren at York seceded from their antient lodge and applied to London for a warrant of constitution. The application was accepted, but instead of being recommended to their Mother Grand Lodge to be restored to favor, these Brethren were encouraged in their revolt and, under the banner of the Grand Lodge in London, opened a second lodge in the city of York. This illegal extension of power offended the Grand Lodge in York and caused a breach that was not healed until 1817 with the formation of a United Grand Lodge of England.

The Grand Lodge of England in London

Today all English Freemasons are told that Freemasonry originated in London in 1717, when four lodges held meetings at four London Taverns: the Goose and Gridiron Ale-House in St. Paul's Churchyard; The Crown in Parker Lane near Drury Lane; the Appletree Tavern in Charles Street, Covent Garden; and the Rummer and Grapes Tavern in Channel Row, Westminster. The longer history of the Grand Lodge in York is rarely mentioned.

The unlikely story currently told is that, on a sudden whim, these four lodges, whose gentlemen members happened to pick up some interesting ideas from their local building sites, decided to join together to create a new Grand Lodge and rule a new order called Freema-

sonry. This new Grand Lodge, it is said, went on to develop the world-wide fraternal organization that is Freemasonry today. Anyone reading the *Masonic Year Book* of the United Grand Lodge of England can be forgiven for believing this story because this official publication contains a ten-page section titled "Outstanding Masonic Events" whose first entry reads as follows: "1717 Grand Lodge convened, Anthony Sayer Grand Master."

All English Freemasons are encouraged to believe that the group calling itself "the premier Masonic Institution" was founded by the casual action of four gentlemen's dining clubs that took up the rituals of the stonemasons' guilds for their own moral betterment. But the image of a group of noble gentlemen wandering around their local building sites, asking stoneworkers if they could please join a trade union to improve their morals, might be lifted from the pages of a comedy script. In any event, in light of the real background to Scotland's experience of Freemasonry, it is totally unlikely.

The reason for this strange cover story makes sense when one realizes that the hereditary Grand Masters of Masons in Scotland had an embarrassing history as viewed through the eyes of English Freemasons. The Sinclair family had supported the crowning of Charles II of Scotland against the wishes of Oliver Cromwell, and Roslin Castle had paid the price for their defiance when General Monck razed it to the ground. Scotland continued to support the Stuart kings against the English, and in 1715 the Scots supported James the Pretender's attempt to regain his crown from the House of Hanover.

By 1717, the Freemasons of London were living in a climate of Jacobite witch-hunting. (The Jacobites were supporters of the deposed Stuart king, James II.) The lodges of England had to have come from somewhere, but the only groups to form lodges in the south of England prior to 1641 were Scottish and took their authority from the Stuart-authorized Schaw Statutes of 1602. Anybody in London with Jacobite sympathies at the time was suspect. London Freemasons were linked to the Scots, who had shown strong animosity toward George I, a Hanoverian, and the four established London lodges were acting on the authority of the Scottish Schaw Statutes (still the main source of Masonic regularity).

For supporters of the Hanoverian monarchy, this was extremely troubling. As no doubt they knew, for many years prior to the 1715 campaign, the Scottish lodges had kept a fund to which all brethren had contributed for the purpose of purchasing weapons "kept and reserved for the defense of the true religion, king and country and for the defence of the ancient city and their privileges therein"

and that they were obliged "to adventure their lives and fortunes in defiance of one and all."

If Londoners wanted to meet as Freemasons, they needed to remove these dangerous Jacobite overtones from their Order. Their problem was that their authority to hold lodges as Freemasons came from the Jacobite Schaw Lodges of Scotland. Their solution was novel if Masonically illegitimate. The Londoners created an alternative source of authority for their activities by bringing together four local lodges, denying their Scottish origins, and forming a new Grand Lodge to govern Freemasonry. Then they courted the Hanoverian royal family, encouraging them to join and eventually lead London Freemasonry. Thus, the Freemasons of London wanted to become loyal Hanoverians, while much of Scotland remained quietly Jacobite, toasting the king only after passing their hands over the glass. (This symbolized loyalty to the king over the water, the deposed James II in France.)

Within six years of forming their new Grand Lodge under Anthony Sayer, London Masons persuaded the Duke of Montagu to become Grand Master. In all the years since, they have had some minor lord, or even, on occasion, a royal prince or king, as their Grand Master. When the original exercise in distancing was planned, the main players probably did not think that their "Grand Lodge" would extend its scope much beyond Westminster and the city of London. But they were successful far beyond these simple ambitions for strangely ironic reasons. They set out to make clear that they had no loyalty to the Scottish Masonic Lodge system, which had deeply rooted support for the Stuart kings and a proclivity to support anti-Hanoverian causes. William Preston, an 18th-century historian of Freemasonry, describes the situation:

JOHN, 2ND DUKE OF MONTAGU

The support and patronage that Freemasonry enjoyed under the Stuart kings became an issue of loyalty under George I, who did not patronise Freemasonry. The minor nobility who had previously joined The Craft melted away. The masons in London and its environs, finding their annual meetings discontinued, resolved to cement under a Grand Master, and to revive the communications and annual festivals of the Society. With this view, the lodges at the Goose and Gridiron in St. Paul's Church-yard, the Crown in Parker's-lane near Drury-lane, the Apple-tree tavern in Charles-street Covent-garden, and the Rummer and Grapes tavern in Channel-row Westminster, the only four lodges in being in the south of England at that time, with some other old brethren, met at the Apple-tree tavern above mentioned in February 1717; and having voted the oldest master-mason then present into the chair, constituted themselves a Grand Lodge pro tempore in due form. At this meeting it was resolved to revive the quarterly communications of the fraternity; and to hold the next annual assembly and feast on the 24th of June, at the Goose and Gridiron in St. Paul's Church-yard (in compliment to the oldest lodge, which then met there) for the purpose of electing a Grand Master among themselves, till they should again have the honour of a noble brother at their head. Accordingly, on St. John the Baptist's day 1717, in the third year of the reign of king

IF THE KING WON'T JOIN, THIS GUY WILL HAVE TO DO.

George I the assembly and feast were held at the said house; when the oldest Master-mason, and Master of a lodge, having taken the chair, a list of proper candidates for the office of Grand Master was produced: and the names being separately proposed, the brethren, by a great majority of hands, elected Mr. Anthony Sayer Grand Master of masons for the ensuing year; who was forthwith invested by the said oldest Master, installed by the Master of the oldest lodge, and duly congratulated by the assembly, who paid him homage.

One was intellectual and seeking to ingratiate itself with Hanoverian society; the other was a group of Stuart-sympathizing Freemasons who enjoyed eating, drinking, and general Masonic merriment.

Both groups wanted the acceptance of a noble Grand Master, but neither had any noble members wishing to stick their necks out to run an Order with a distinct whiff of Jacobitism. So they made do with

WELL, THEY HAVEN'T KILLED SAYER YET...

a gentleman who was down on his luck, Anthony Sayer, a member of the Lodge at the Apple Tree Tavern (now the Lodge of Fortitude and Old Cumberland No. 12). Before Sayer's election, being a Grand Master of Freemasonry was considered risky in light of known Jacobite activities on the part of London brethren and strong memories of the 1715 uprising. But once a year passed without the Hanoverian loyalty of the new Grand Lodge being questioned, Sayer was replaced for two terms by George Payne, a civil servant who had worked in King George I's Exchequer. (Payne went on to become Secretary to the King's Tax Office.) His main contribution was to compile a set of regulations for governing the London lodges to keep them free of any suspicion of Jacobitism. Sayer was downgraded to Senior Grand Warden and then paid to act as Tyler (door guard) of the Old King's Arms Lodge.

As Grand Master, Payne took as his wardens John Theophilus Desaguliers and John, second Duke of Montagu. Montagu had been

JOHN THEOPHILUS DESAGULIERS

introduced to Freemasonry by Desaguliers. The Reverend John Theophilus Desaguliers was a clergyman, chaplain to the Duke of Chandos, and a natural scientist who assisted Sir Isaac Newton in his experiments. Desaguliers had been made a member of the Royal Society in 1714 and studied civil engineering. He met Montagu through the Royal Society, which encouraged wealthy noblemen to join and support it financially. Montagu had followed his father by becoming a Fellow of the Royal Society in 1717.

Desaguliers designed an impressive system of water supply pipes for the Duke of Chandos's ancestral home, Canons Park, and when the Lord Provost of Edinburgh saw the water works, he invited Desaguliers to visit Edinburgh to advise on setting up a water and sewage system for the city. While visiting in 1721, Desaguliers attended a meeting of the Lodge of Edinburgh. According to lodge minutes, the Brethren found him qualified on all points of Masonry and received him as a Brother.

Despite their attempts to distance themselves from Scottish Masonry, the brethren of the new Grand Lodge in London were still practicing the Stuart Freemasonry they were attempting to disown. Had they really invented something completely new, Desaguliers would not have been able to prove himself a Mason to his longstanding Scottish Brethren.

John, second Duke of Montagu, had impeccable Hanoverian credentials as a Grand Master for the new Grand Lodge, with its aspirations of Hanoverian acceptance. He had been High Constable at the coronation of George I in 1714 and had been knighted by the king in 1719. But his mother-in-law, Sarah Churchill, Duchess of Marlborough, testified that he was fond of practical jokes; as she wrote in her diary: "All my son-in-law's talents lie in things natu-ral to boys of fifteen, and he is about two and fifty: to get people into his gardens and wet them with squirts, to invite people to his house and put things into their beds to make them itch, and twenty other such pretty fancies."

Montagu must have enjoyed the Masonic rituals. Perhaps that is how Desaguliers enticed him to be made a Mason and later to become Grand Master. He lived and entertained in style in Montagu House, Bloomsbury, and had no heirs. After his death, his dukedom became extinct, and his impressive house became the British Museum.

The Grand Lodge of London looked set on the road to social acceptability under Montagu, but, apart from its dinning-club faction, proved boring. The jolly diners saw a chance in 1723, when Montagu was given the islands of St. Lucia and St. Vincent in the West Indies by King George. He filled seven ships with settlers and supplies to establish colonies in his new overseas holdings. Unfortunately, the French took St. Lucia and drove out Montagu's governor. The colony on St. Vincent then fought off the French, but the whole affair cost Montagu a fortune and took him away from his Masonry activities. The dining club faction thus put forward Philip, Duke of Wharton, as Grand Master, and he was quite a different proposition from the staid Montagu.

PHILIP, DUKE OF WHARTON

The founders of the Grand Lodge in London had been associated with the Jacobites and found the new arrangements a major departure from the sociable eating and drinking club they had known. Montagu and Desaguliers had been of an intellectual inclination and not much given to jovial dining. The Duke of Wharton, by contrast, had been a suspected Jacobite and president of the disreputable and disbanded Hell-Fire Club. After the demise of that group, Wharton was seeking a new venue for eating, drinking, and general merrymaking. Freemasonry, with its tradition of the Festive Board, must have seemed the ideal vehicle.

With George I's High Constable, the Duke of Montagu, as Grand Master, the number of members had grown to over 2,000. Under the Duke of Wharton, however, the Craft risked turning into little more than a London dining and drinking club while still denying its long history under the Stuart monarchs.

Wharton's success in seizing the Grand Mastership put Desaguliers' dream of Hanoverian acceptability at risk. And for a while the battle got dirty. When confronted by Desaguliers, Wharton threatened to withdraw all of his supporters from the Grand Lodge and leave it nonviable. In an effort to counterbalance Wharton's infamous reputation, Desaguliers was made his Deputy Grand Master.

An unknown supporter of Montagu's responded by publishing a hoax advertisement announcing the formation of a competing body called the Gormagons, with the idea that such a ludicrous parody of Freemasonry would discredit Wharton and ridicule his position. Wharton lasted just a year before the Grand Lodge dumped him in favor of the staid and solid Earl of Dalkeith.

By separating themselves from their Scottish roots, the Masons of London were slowly rebuilding the popularity and standing of

Freemasonry in London's Hanoverian Society. But there had been a price to pay for this acceptance. The London Masons had had to disown their real history, losing touch with 200 years of tradition marked by ancient constitutions and statutes. They had an Order whose practices had been refined by nearly ten generations of selective reinforcement but had to pretend they were newborn. They couldn't draw on tradition to provide authority, so they needed something to replace their lost history.

The man whom Desaguliers turned to for a solution was a Master Mason from the Lodge of Aberdeen. He was the Reverend James Anderson, a Presbyterian Minister to Swallow Street Chapel in London and personal Chaplain to the Earl of Buchan. In his double personae as a member of the Lodge of Aberdeen and a confident of the Earl of Buchan, Anderson was steeped in the mythical history of Freemasonry that he had learned from his mother lodge.

Anderson's Constitutions

For four generations, the family of Rev. Anderson had been members of the Lodge of Aberdeen. He came to London as chaplain to the Earl of Buchan in the early 1700s. Anderson was a Scottish Freemason who had served as Master of the Lodge of Aberdeen—a fact that would not have struck sparks of joy in the hearts of the loyally Hanoverian Grand Officers of the new Grand Lodge of London. The Earl of Buchan was a powerful figure in Scottish Freemasonry, as his family were claimed to be early Masters of Lodge Mother Kilwinning, one of the oldest lodges in Scotland. It is based in the town of Ayr, alongside the grounds of Kilwinning Abbey, and is called the

Mother Lodge of Scotland. Its main claim to fame was through its patron, the Earl of Buchan.

The Earls of Buchan were showcased in a newly popularized mythical history of Freemasonry that had been put forward to support the formation of the Royal Order of Scotland (a Masonic Order that keeps an empty chair waiting for the true King of Scots, James VII, or James II of England, to return as its Grand Master). It is based on a Masonic myth about an intervention by Knights Templar at the Battle of Bannockburn in which the Earls of Buchan played a part. According to that myth...

On the 24th June, 1314, Robert Bruce, King of Scotland, instituted, after the battle of Bannockburn, the Order of St. Andrew of the Thistle, to which was afterwards united with that of Heredom for the sake of the Scottish Masons, who composed a part of the 30,000 men with whom he had fought the English army consisting of 100,000. He formed the Royal Grand Lodge of the Order of Heredom at Kilwinning, reserving to himself and his successors—through his youngest son, the Earl of Buchan—forever the title of Grand Master.

In the context of the fevered politics of Hanoverian London in the early 18th century and within the Jacobite Masonic circles of the Royal Order of Scotland, the patronage of the Earl of Buchan (whose ancestral home was just north of Aberdeen) carried great weight. For the newly formed Grand Lodge in London, it would have been a link to

be denied at all costs. So why was the personal chaplain of such a totemic Jacobite figure as the Earl of Buchan invited to regularize the newly formed Grand Lodge?

Anderson brought something more than dodgy Jacobite political connections to the aspirations of the new Grand Lodge. For at least four generations, his family had been members of the Lodge of Aberdeen. He had learned the verbal teachings of that lodge from his father and grandfathers as well as from his lodge brethren. So he was familiar with the ancient statutes and looked with great affection at his great-grand-

father's introduction to the 1670 Mark Book of the Lodge of Aberdeen, which referred to "James Anderson, Glazier and Mason and writer of this book".

Desaguliers saw a need to restore the traditional history, which had been lost by denying the Scottish heritage, so he asked James Anderson to create a set of constitutions to make sure that the new organization was not derailed by the followers of Wharton. But this strategy carried some risk. He needed to be able to claim a traditional heritage for the Order that didn't link it to the Stuart Jacobite cause.

Anderson did a great service to the Craft by restoring its traditional history, taking the mythical origins of the Craft from the verbal tradition of the Jacobite-tainted Lodge of Aberdeen and implanting it into the struggling Hanoverian Grand Lodge in London. He thereby distanced the London Masons from the Jacobite-tainted Masonic supporters of the King of Scots at Bannockburn.

Desaguliers persuaded Anderson to retell the mythical history of the Craft, which had been developed in Aberdeen, so as to provide an ancient lineage for the Order while keeping it clear of the links to the Jacobite-inspired Royal Order of Scotland.

In 1738, Anderson said that he had been instructed to "digest" the old histories and rewrite them in a suitable form for modern use. Desaguliers, from his time to Edinburgh, was aware of the various mythical histories of the Craft taught in Scotland and persuaded Anderson to graft the least politically risky part of that history onto the newly formed Grand Lodge in London. In this way, he could restore some of the prestige that had been lost with the fall from grace of the traditional royal patrons of Freemasonry, the Stuart monarchy.

In 1710, Anderson had served as Minister at the Presbyterian Kirk in Swallow Street London. A Provincial Grand Lodge of the Royal Order of Scotland had been founded in London in 1696 and, until

1730, continued to meet in the Thistle and Crown on Chandos Street, Charing Cross, not half a mile from Bro. Anderson's Kirk. At their meetings, they kept an empty chair inviting the return of the true King of Scots.

As a Scot, a Freemason, and the Chaplin of the Earl of Buchan, Anderson knew what was going on. Still, he must have wondered how he could hope to draw on the authority of the Masonic origin legend to support the Hanoverian hopefuls of the Grand Lodge in London. Times were difficult for Jacobite supporters of the exiled Stuart kings, but Anderson proved to be resourceful, inspired, and well-versed in the alternative strands of mythical Masonic history that kept away from the Jacobite links of the Earls of Buchan. He created the cover story, still told today, of the inspiration of the local trade guilds.

Grand Lodges in Scotland and Ireland

Not all Masons accepted that the Hanoverian-supporting London Masons should be allowed to rule Freemasonry everywhere. Soon after the founding of the Grand Lodge in London in 1717, Grand Lodges were formed in Munster and Dublin to protect the interests of their largely Jacobite Brethren. The self-ruling, warrant-issuing lodges in Scotland saw no need to act, but dissatisfaction with the English Hanoverian monarchy was growing.

MANY SOCIETIES WERE FORMED IN SCOTLAND TO PROMOTE THE INTERESTS OF THE JACOBITE "KING OVER THE WATER" AND HIS HEIR.

Among these was the Royal Company of Archers of Edinburgh, whose parades, competitions, and shows of strength were bothering the insecure government of King George I by about 1724. The threat posed by the exiled Stuart Pretender caused so much concern that when the names of an inner group known as the Sovereign Bodyguard of Scotland were published by an English sympathizer, the Masons of Scotland admitted that their hereditary Grand Master Mason was a brigadier of this Jacobite Royal Company of Archers.

The actions of the Hanoverian Freemasons in England and Wales, along with the formation of a Grand Lodge in Ireland, started to worry the lodges of Scotland. To make sure that Wales didn't form its own National Grand Lodge, the London Grand Lodge persuaded Hugh Warburton to accept the newly created role of Provincial Grand Master of Wales. This made the separate country of Wales a province of England (a step something like making the United States a province of Canada). This strange arrangement still irritates many brethren in Welsh lodges.

A system of control and patronage was developed to ensure that all lodges complied with the edicts of the gentlemen Freemasons of London. The appointment of the Scottish Earl of Strathmore and Lord Crawford as Grand Masters of London Freemasonry suggested that it would not be long before a Scottish Freemason would be found to call himself the Provincial Grand Master of Scotland, as a province of England.

The Lodges of Mother Kilwinning and Scoon and Perth did not think this was a real threat, but the Edinburgh lodges took it seriously. And they came up with a solution. They decided to elect a Grand Lodge of their own to administer their affairs issue warrants on their behalf, and protect their interests. They needed a suitable

WILLIAM ST. CLAIR

Grand Master Mason but the Schaw Statutes, on which they based their authority, left them no choice.

William St Clair, the nineteenth Baron of Roslin, had to be their hereditary Patron. Unfortunately he wasn't a Freemason, just a member of the Jacobite Company of Archers. In order for the plan to be carried out, therefore, he was initiated into Freemasonry on May 8, 1736. On June 2, he was made a Master Mason, and on December 30 installed as the First Grand Master Mason of Scotland. St Clair immediately renounced all his assumed hereditary rights of Patronage and instituted the system of election of Officers of Grand Lodge that still protects the rights and privileges of Scottish Freemasons to this day.

Thus, by 1736, there were four Grand Lodges in the British Isles: one in York, one in London, one in Dublin, and one in Edinburgh. From this start, Freemasonry began to spread throughout the world.

THE SPREAD OF FREEMASONRY

CHARLES RADCLIFFE

THE FIRST LODGE TO BE established outside the British Isles was located in Paris. It was opened by the brother of James Radcliffe, the Jacobite Earl of Derwentwater, who had been executed for treason against the Hanoverians in 1716. The brother, Charles Radcliffe, who inherited James's title, fled to Paris and founded this first recorded lodge of Freemasons in France in 1725. Charles, Earl of Derwentwater, was also secretary to Prince Charles Edward Stuart (Bonnie Prince Charlie), and the lodge in Paris consisted entirely of Stuart sympathizers and supporters of James II. This Earl of Derwentwater was eventually captured during the 1745 rebellion and beheaded.

Freemasonry in France

By 1730, there were five lodges in Paris: *Loge St. Thomas* (later renamed *Louis D'Argent*), *Loge Bussy, Loge Aumont, Loge Parfaite Union*, and *Loge Bernouville.*

The first Grand Master Mason of France was the Duc d'Antin. He was initiated in 1737, at Aubigny, by the Duke

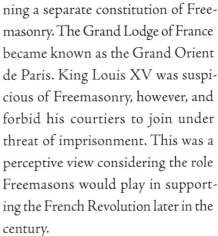

of Richmond, a Past Grand Master of English Freemasonry. D'Antin was authorized by the English Grand Lodge to form new lodges in France, beginning a separate constitution of Freemasonry. The Grand Lodge of France became known as the Grand Orient de Paris. King Louis XV was suspicious of Freemasonry, however, and forbid his courtiers to join under threat of imprisonment. This was a perceptive view considering the role Freemasons would play in supporting the French Revolution later in the century.

The earliest references to Scottish Rite degrees in France date between the 1715 and 1745 Jacobite Rebellions. The Scottish Rite is a popular group of higher Masonic degrees beyond the three craft degrees in the United States. The Masons who worked these degrees were known as *Maitres Ecossais,* or Scottish Masons. These

CHEVALIER RAMSAY

higher degrees are associated with a native of Ayr—where Lodge Mother Kilwinning had been established—named Chevalier Ramsay. Born in 1686, Ramsay by 1724 served as tutor to the two sons of James II of England, then living in exile in France. (One of the sons was the young Bonnie Prince Charlie, who would lead a 1745 expedition to try to regain the throne of Great Britain.)

In 1737, Ramsay published a story about a union between Freemasonry and the Knights of Jerusalem that dated back to the time of the Crusades. Ramsay's *Oration*, as it was titled, appeared in a journal called *L'Almanach de Cocus*. Ramsay also described an early—but otherwise unrecorded—story of the Lodge at Kilwinning, in which he claimed that James, Lord Steward of Scotland, was Master in 1286. This was untrue, obviously, as Freemasonry did not even exist at the time. Ramsay's motive seems to have been to link the mythical history of Freemasonry, concerning Israel's King David, the first divinely appointed king, and his son, King Solomon, to King James II, who, he implied, should also be ruling England by divine right.

Ramsay was a Jacobite, a trusted tutor to Bonnie Prince Charlie, and a member of the lodge founded by the Earl of Derwentwater, who had fled to France with James II. That lodge, the first in France, met at Hure's Tavern on Rue des Boucheries in Paris.

In 1730, by permission of King George II, Ramsay visited England and was made a

Fellow of the Royal Society. According the honor was Sir Isaac New-ton, the Society's president. Ramsay had no obvious scientific quali-fications, except that he was a Freemason. While in England, he also joined the Horn Lodge (now known as the Royal Somerset House and Inverness Lodge No. 4).

Benjamin Franklin, the Provincial Grand Master of Pennsylvania, traveled to Paris after signing the Declaration of Independence in 1776 to serve as ambassador and seek the military support of the French. While in Paris, Franklin worked with local Freemasons to establish a bond of affiliation and mutual recognition between the Lodges of France and the Lodges of Pennsylvania. Indeed he was made an hon-orary member of *Loge Des IX Soeurs* and earned the friendship of as many French Freemasons as possible.

In early 1778, with the Continental Army under George Washing-ton turning the tide of battle against British forces, Franklin was able to begin negotiating in earnest with the French regime of Louis XIV.

In February of that year, delegates of the two nations signed a treaty that established a defensive military alliance and granted official French recognition of an independent United States. That April, Franklin initiated the great French philosopher Voltaire as a Freemason in *Loge Des IX Soeur* in Paris. Sadly, in May of the following year,

he gave a eulogy at Voltaire's funeral. The culmination of Franklin's years in France was the 1783 Treaty of Paris, which ended the war of independence against Britain and was part of a broader peace among the European powers. To honor his work in building friendship between the United States and France, Franklin was made a Venerable Officer of the *Grand Orient de Paris*. His activities and relationships as a Freemason were critical to his success.

Freemasonry in the British Empire
Now let us return to the early days of the Grand Lodge of England. In

FRANCIS I

1727, it issued the first recorded warrant for an overseas lodge, in Gibraltar. This was closely followed by permission to hold a lodge in St. Bernard's Street, Madrid. Freemasonry was spreading like wildfire, and by 1728 the London Grand Lodge started to establish itself throughout the British Empire. It granted a deputation to George Pomfret to establish a lodge in Calcutta and appointed Provincial Grand Masters for Lower Saxony in Germany and New Jersey in America.

In 1730, the first foreign prince of royal blood was initiated—Francis, Duke of Lorraine and Grand Duke of Tuscany. He was initiated by the Earl of Chesterfield at a special Lodge convened at The Hague, where he received the first two degrees of Masonry. The duke was later raised to the third degree at the home of Prime Minister Robert Walpole, at a lodge also chaired by the Earl of Chesterfield. The worldwide spread of the Craft continued. That same year, the English Grand Lodge issued deputations to form lodges in Russia, Spain, and Flanders.

The Order was fast becoming a stylish dining club for nobility, holding its first country Feast at Hampstead on June 24, 1730. Cards of invitation were sent to a number of noble brethren. The range of influence of the London Grand Lodge was growing as well. By 1733, a total of 53 lodges were represented at its Annual Communication. At this meeting, several new regulations were confirmed with respect to the operations of the Charity Committee, including the right to hear its own complaints before they were brought before Grand Lodge. Also at this meeting, a collection was taken to be distributed among distressed Masons and to encourage them to found of a new colony in Georgia. During that year, deputations were granted to open lodges in Hamburg, Germany, and Holland.

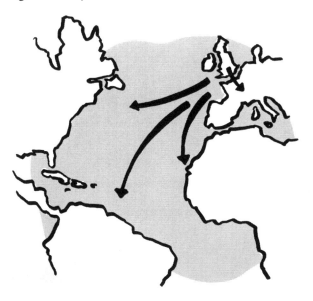

In 1738, James Anderson published his revised book of constitutions, described in the previous chapter. It was this reworking of the history of the Craft that has caused some authors to attribute to him the creation of Craft Masonry. At about this time, regulations were introduced to the effect that if a lodge ceased to meet for more than 12 months, then it would be erased from the list and lose its seniority. It was also established at this time that all future Grand Masters would be elected from the Grand Stewards' Lodge, so as to encourage gentlemen to join that one. More controversial were resolutions concerning what were described as illegal Masonic conventions. The Grand Lodge in London also started to encroach on the territory of the Grand Lodge in York by warranting lodges in Lancashire, Durham, and Northumberland. These actions reduced the friendly intercourse between the two Grand Lodges.

Meanwhile, warrants were issued to hold lodges in Aubigny in France (as already mentioned), Lisbon in Portugal, Savannah in

Georgia, South America, and Gambay in West Africa. Provincial Grand Masters were appointed to New England, South Carolina, and the Cape Coast in Africa. In 1737, Rev. Dr. Desaguliers initiated Frederick, the Prince of Wales, at a lodge convened for that purpose at Kew. Later that year, Frederick was passed to the second degree and then raised to the degree of a Master Mason. He was being groomed for a future Grand Mastership.

At the main meeting of the Grand Lodge that year, a total of 60 lodges were represented, and Provincial Grand Masters were appointed for Montserrat, Geneva, the Coast of Africa, New York, and the Islands of America. Two further Provinces came into being in 1738—the Caribbean Islands and the Province of Yorkshire West Riding. This was considered yet another encroachment on the rights of the Grand Lodge in York, which widened the breach with their London counterparts and resulted in a total breakdown of relations.

New lodges continued to spring up on the Continent, some founded by Hanoverian Masons and others by refugee Jacobites. All lodges welcomed brother Masons without regard to religion or politics, so they became sources of intelligence for both sides of the Jacobite struggle. Unfortunately for James II, now known as the Old Pretender, Prime Minister Walpole was far better at the spying game than the Jacobites. The king came to regard the Freemason's lodges that followed his court, first at St. Germain and later in Rome, as threats to his chances to regain the crown of Britain and persuaded the Pope to denounce them.

Freemasonry in Germany

The Germans took to Freemasonry with great enthusiasm. In 1718, a year after the formation of the Grand Lodge of England, a lodge was formed in Hamburg by a Dr. Jaenisch, who had been initiated in London. In 1729, the Duke of Norfolk, then serving as Grand Master Mason of England, promoted this lodge to become the Grand Lodge of Hamburg and made its Master a Provincial Grand Master under the English Constitution. The Hamburg Lodge later became known as Lodge Absalom.

In 1738, the Worshipful Master of the Hamburg Lodge initiated Frederick the Great of Prussia, then the Crown Prince. His father, King Frederick William I, was violently opposed to Freemasonry and had forbidden any of his subjects to take part in its meetings. Crown Prince Frederick, however, was fascinated by the Order and asked Count Albert Wolfgang of Lippe-Buckeburg, a member of the Hamburg Lodge, to arrange for him to be secretly initiated. Count Albert arranged a meeting at a hotel in Brunswick on August 14, 1738, where Crown Prince

Frederick was made a Mason and became a member of the Lodge of Hamburg. He held secret lodge meetings at Rheinsberg and soon progressed to Worshipful Master.

After the death of his father on May 31, 1740, and his ascension to the throne, Frederick made Freemasonry fashionable in German Society. He announced that he was a Brother Mason and set up a Masonic lodge in Berlin called the Lodge of the Three Globes. It became the first Grand Lodge of Germany and was warranted by the king, who became its Grand Master. Frederick continued to support Freemasonry until his death 1786, by which time the Craft was firmly established in Germany.

Fortunes changed when Adolf Hitler came to power in 1933 and accused Freemasonry of being part of a worldwide Judeo- Masonic Conspiracy. The Ten German Regional Grand Lodges were dissolved, their Temples destroyed, and their ritual books burned. Many Masons were sent to concentration camps and died there. During the time of Nazi persecution, Masons in Germany adopted the symbol of the forget-me-not flower to identify themselves to brethren. When the Regional Grand Lodges of Germany were reestablished after the

end of World War II, the forget-me-not was officially adopted as an emblem of Masons who had survived the years of darkness under Nazi oppression. It is still worn by German Masons today as a badge of identity.

The Spread of the Scottish Rite

IT WAS IN THE AMERICAN COLONIES THAT THE HIGHER DEGREES OF THE SCOTTISH RITE BECAME POPULAR.

In 1761, the Grand Lodge of France issued a patent to a merchant named Etienne (Stephen) Morin to spread the Scottish Rite in America. Morin was made Grand Inspector of the New World and authorized to create Inspectors in all places where these degrees were not already established. By May 31, 1801, he had established the Supreme Council of the Thirty-Three Degrees for the United States of America in Charleston, South Carolina. His instructions were to promote and encourage the working of those degrees.

In the following year, the Supreme Council issued a circular to all the Grand Lodges of the World claiming that the origin of Freemasonry dated to the beginning of the world. The document went on to describe the development of the Craft up to its own formation and declared itself the keeper of Secret Constitutions, which had existed from Time Immemorial. This established yet another mythical history of Freemasonry, which now claimed Adam as the first Freemason.

The nine founding members of the first Supreme Council, which issued warrants to form other Supreme Councils, were:

1. John Mitchell
2. Frederick Dalcho
3. Emanuel de la Motta
4. Abraham Alexander
5. Thomas Bartholomew Bowen
6. Israel De Lieben
7. Dr. Isaac Auld
8. Moses Clava Levy
9. Dr. James Moultrie

Some Masons in Ireland and an English group known as the Baldwyn Encampment of Bristol worked versions of the Scottish Rite under warrants that originated from Scotland. The Supreme Council of Scotland constituted itself on June 4, 1845, under the leadership Dr. George Walker Arnott. The next year, this body acted to legitimize the Supreme Council of Charleston by admitting its officers as members of the 31st, 32nd and 33rd degrees of the Supreme Council for Scotland and agreeing to warrant its activities. In this way, the two competing councils for Scottish Rite Freemasonry came to work together to spread the Scottish Rite in America.

Thus, by the mid-18th century, barely 30 years after the establishment of the Grand Lodge of England, Freemasonry had a firm footing in the remoter parts of the European continent, as well as India, Africa, and the Americas.

This was the period when new mythical histories were created and the embarrassing Scottish Jacobite roots of the Order were conveniently forgotten.

THE GROWTH OF FRATERNALISM IN THE UNITED STATES AND BEYOND

JONATHAN BELCHER, BORN IN BOSTON IN 1681, was the first American Freemason. He was actually initiated into an English lodge in 1704 and became the colonies' first Freemason when he returned to Boston in 1705. His son Andrew followed him into Masonry, but unfortunately we know nothing more about him.

JONATHAN BELCHER

The Military Lodges

Freemasonry was carried to North America by military lodges attached to various British regiments. There is not much documentation

regarding the early lodges in America, as the lodge Charter and Minute Book was kept—and sometimes lost—by regimental commanders. Often a lodge would be run in the form a tabletop lodge. A special cloth showed the main symbols and miniature Tracing Boards so it could be carried in a small chest. Typically only the officers of the regiment were members, but, if they stayed in a town for long periods, they would initiate local men. When the regiment moved on, the civilian Masons would form an ad hoc lodge of their own. In this way, Freemasonry spread across the North American colonies.

The Grand Lodge of Ireland issued the first warrant to a traveling military lodge, the First British Foot Regiment, in 1732. Soon the Grand Lodge of Scotland and both Grand Lodges of England also issued charters to military Lodges. By 1755, there were a total of 29 official traveling military lodges, as well as three naval lodges formed under the Grand Lodge of England. Many of the new European Grand Lodges also created military lodges, but they were linked to a fixed meeting place. They did not travel or meet overseas and so played no part in taking Freemasonry to America.

On July 30, 1733, Bro. Henry Price, a tailor who had immigrated to America ten years earlier, called a meeting of local Freemasons at the Bunch of Grapes Tavern in King Street (now called State Street) in Boston. Price was a member of Britannic Lodge No. 33, which met at the Rainbow Tavern in London. He had just come from a visit to London and carried

HENRY PRICE

BUNCH OF GRAPES
TAVERN

with him a commission to form a Provincial Grand Lodge of New England. Price became its Grand Master, made Andrew Belcher (the son of Jonathon) his Deputy, and appointed Thomas Kennel and John Quan as his Grand Wardens.

A lodge was opened, and eight local men were initiated into Freemasonry. The newly initiated Masons immediately petitioned Grand Master Price to be allowed to form a lodge, and he agreed. The first regular Masonic lodge in America, to be known as St. John's Lodge, was born that night. In 1734, Grand Master Price authorized Benjamin Franklin to issue warrants to form lodges in Pennsylvania, and Freemasonry gradually became established in America, as a province of England. In the decades that followed, however, issues of colonial rule caused problems that resulted in a whole new, Masonically inspired Constitution for an independent country. It would be called the United States of America.

The spark that ignited the conflict was a Masonic tea party in Boston.

The Boston Tea Party

In 1773, the East India Company, England's great maritime trade power, was warehousing great piles of tea imported from Asia that nobody wanted to buy. The royally chartered company persuaded the British Government to grant it a monopoly to sell tea to the colonies, including those in North America. To add insult to injury for the colonists, the Tea Act passed by Parliament that March forced Americans to buy only authorized and taxed tea. The colonists of Massachusetts had bristled at a series of arbitrary taxes imposed by the British on sugar and other basic goods. Indeed, tensions had been mounting for some time before three ships laden with poor-quality, highly taxed tea arrived in Boston Harbor in late November and nearly December.

The Masonic Lodge of St. Andrews met in the Green Dragon Tavern in Boston, the same building where the Grand Lodge of Massachusetts convened. The Grand Master of Massachusetts, Dr. Joseph Warren, was a member of St. Andrew's Lodge, as were silversmith Paul Revere and merchant John Hancock. The lodge members were known to sing a song, popular among Patriots of the clandestine Sons of Liberty group, called "Rally Mohawks." Its words went as follows:

Rally, Mohawks! Bring out your axes,
And tell King George we'll pay no taxes
On his foreign tea!

His threats are vain, and vain to think
To force our girls and wives to drink
His vile Bohea! [name for poor-quality tea]

Then rally boys, and hasten on
To meet our Chiefs at the Green Dragon.
Our Warren's there, and bold Revere,
With hands to do and words to cheer,
For Liberty and Laws!

Our country's "braves" and firm defenders
Shall ne'er be left by true North-Enders,
Fighting Freedom's cause!
Then rally boys and hasten on
To meet our Chiefs at the Green Dragon.

The brethren of St. Andrews Lodge argued that "taxation without representation" was tyranny, made worse by enforcing a monopoly of poor-quality tea. No one is sure who the Mohawks were, but they shared the views of St. Andrew's Brethren and decided to do something about it.

On the night of December 16, 1773, a group of about 60 men in painted faces, calling themselves Mohawks, met at the Green Dragon Tavern. Together they went down to the docks where the tea ships were moored, clambered on board, dumped 90,000 pounds of tea into the harbor.

On October 23, more than a month before the three ships arrived in Boston Harbor, Brethren Joseph Warren and Paul Revere, of St. Andrew's Lodge published a resolution "To oppose the vending of any tea sent by the East India Company" and pledged to support it with their lives and fortunes.

On November 3, Bro. William Molineux of St. Andrew's Lodge posted a notice on the Liberty Tree near the Boston Common, a rallying point for the Patriot cause. The notice was signed by the Sons of Liberty and demanded that the Consignees of the Tea resign as agents of the East India Company. The Consignees ignored the notice, and Bros. Molineux and Warren, along with 300 supporters, marched

on the Customs House to challenge them. After ripping the doors from their hinges, they demanded an immediate resignation. The tea agents refused and fled to Fort William, on an island in the harbor, to seek British military protection. The consignees of New York, Philadelphia, and Charleston all resigned, and the tea ships at those ports were forced back to England, as there was nobody to receive delivery

of the tea or pay the taxes. The consignees in Boston, however, who were sons of Royal Governor Thomas Hutchinson, refused to resign. They knew if they held out until December 17, the disputed tea would be forfeited to their father, who could sell it, recover the taxes, and make a tidy profit.

At the time, there was a committee of tradesmen in Boston known as the

Selectmen, led by Bro. John Hancock of St. Andrew's Lodge. Hancock was not only one of the richest men in the British Colonies, but also colonel of the Army Cadet Force, a youth training organization. Governor Hutchinson put Hancock and his military cadets in charge of the security of the Boston tea ships.

One of the three ships moored in Boston Harbor, called the *Eleanor*, was owned by John Rowe, the Worshipful Master of St. John's Lodge. Rowe offered to try to persuade the Consignees to resign and the Governor to return the ships and their cargoes back to England. But Rowe was unable to change the minds of either the Consignees or the Governor, who were too concerned about their profits to back down.

PAUL
REVERE

On November 28, the *Dartmouth*, a tea ship owned by a Quaker named Francis Rotch arrived in Boston and tied up at dockside. Joseph Warren called a town meeting, while Paul Revere and his men mounted guard at quayside to stop the ship from unloading. The following evening, according to the minutes of St. Andrew's, the lodge had to be adjourned due to lack of attendance. This was not surprising, since many of the Brethren had gone to the Town Meeting. At that gathering, a notice was sent to the Consignees denouncing their failure to resign and threatening further unspecified action.

The situation remained deadlocked. Revere's guards would not allow the ships to be unloaded; the consignees would not resign and remained liable for the customs tax before the ships could be moved. Then Governor Hutchinson ordered a blockade of the harbor so the ships could not leave. Unless the cargo was unloaded and the tax paid by December 17, the tea would forfeit to the governor, who was bound and determined to sell it.

The minutes of St. Andrew's for the night of December 16 show that most of the brethren missed another lodge, as they—along with 5,000 other Bostonians—attended a fateful gathering at the Old South Meeting House organized by Dr. Warren, Samuel Adams, and others. Francis Rotch was summoned before the meeting and asked if he would return the *Dartmouth* to England with the tea. He said he would not, as this would bring financial ruin. Then he was asked if he intended to unload the cargo at Griffin's Wharf. He said he could not, as he was not allowed to. The meeting broke up with the deadlock unresolved.

That night, after the meeting ended, the group of Patriots disguised as Mohawk Indians dumped the tea into Boston Harbor. John

Hancock's Military Cadets stood back and did nothing. The ship's crew either went below or helped bring up the tea for the Mohawks to throw overboard.

The many Bostonians who had come from the meeting stood in silence and watched. Their silent witness made it impossible for the admiral on board a British warship in the bay to intervene.

The colonial Attorney General placed five members of the St. Andrew's Lodge on a list of men suspected of treason, with Grand Master Joseph Warren at the top. Despite the crowd of bystanders, however, no witnesses came forward and the charges of treason were dropped for lack of evidence. Governor Hutchinson was recalled to England in disgrace, and his sons were forced to repay the money they had made from exploiting the tea monopoly. General Thomas Gage was made the new Governor, with orders to identify and convict those responsible for the Boston Tea Party, as it was now known. He never found enough evidence to bring charges.

Benjamin Franklin, the Grand Master Mason of Pennsylvania, was in London when news of the tea party arrived. He offered to pay for the tea himself, to save his Boston brethren from being put on trial.

No one paid for the tea in the end because Parliament closed the port of Boston, cut off trade with the colonies, and sent in troops.

The War of Independence

The discontent of British colonists in North America, seething under the arbitrary, autocratic rule of a distant king, culminated in the Continental Congress and its bold step toward independence during the summer of 1776. The delegates recognized that absolute power vested in a single authority is easy to abuse, and they came to agree that such abuse had to be challenged and abolished. The document they drafted and ratified to state the case against this form of rule was called the Declaration of Independence.

Of the 56 men who signed the Declaration of Independence on July 4, 1776, a total of 18 were Masons. All were well versed in democratic principles through their membership in Freemasonry. The *self-evident truths* that must be considered when a group of people decides to govern themselves, according the first line of the Declaration, had been part of Masonic teaching for some 300 years.

We hold these truths to be self-evident, that all men are created equal, that they are endowed by their Creator with certain unalienable rights that among these are life, liberty, and the pursuit of happiness. That to secure these rights, governments are instituted among men, deriving their just powers from the consent of the governed. That whenever any form of government becomes destructive to these ends, it is the right of the people to alter or to abolish it, and to institute new government, laying its foundation on such principles and organizing its powers in such form, as to them shall seem most likely to affect their safety and happiness.

The founders of United States knew that to declare self-rule, they had to establish an intellectual basis for self-government. Among them was a sizable minority trained in the Masonic principles of running a lodge as laid down by William Schaw in the late 16th century. According to those rules, readers will recall, the overall Master will be supported by two other officers responsible for different aspects of governance. The Master makes the rules, the Senior Warden enforces them, and the Junior Warden makes sure they are applied fairly. Although the Master takes the lead in lodge affairs, there is no absolute ruler. The three officers work together to meet the responsibilities of lodge governance. Perhaps most important to the founders of the United States was the fact that the Master is elected by members. Thus, the Declaration of Independence drew on another basic Masonic symbol for its *raison d'etre*—the ballot box, used to elect candidates and Masters of Freemasonry just as U.S. citizens elect their president and legislators.

The path trod by the British colonies in North America from declaring independence to establishing a constitutional government is one of the great journeys in the history of democratic society. Not always recognized in the historical accounts of that journey is the direct inspiration of Masonic principles. For indeed the three-part system of checks and balances conceived by the founders of the new American republic—consisting of a president, legislature, and Supreme Court—bears remarkable resemblance to the threefold system of Masonic governance, and not by accident. The result was the most innovative and influential national constitution ever written, imbued with Masonic principles that made it a living, flexible document.

The 18 Masons who signed the Declaration of Independence:

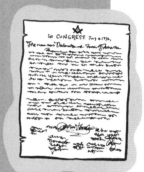

- Josiah Bartlett, *King Solomon's Lodge, Massachusetts*

- William Ellery, *St. Andrew's Lodge, Boston*

- Benjamin Franklin, *St. John's Lodge, Philadelphia*

- Elbridge Gerry, *Philanthropic Lodge, Massachusetts*

- Lyman Hall, *Solomon's Lodge, Georgia*

- John Hancock, *St. Andrew's Lodge, Boston*

- Joseph Hewes, *Hanover Lodge, North Carolina*

- William Hooper, *Hanover Lodge, North Carolina*

- Philip Livingston, *Holland Lodge, New York*

- Thomas McKean, *Perseverance Lodge, Pennsylvania*

- Thomas Nelson, Jr., *Yorktown Lodge, Virginia*

- Robert Treat Paine, *Grand Lodge of Massachusetts*

- John Penn, *Unanimity Lodge, North Carolina*

- Roger Sherman, *lodge unknown*

- Richard Stockton, *St. John's Lodge, New Jersey*

- Matthew Thornton, *British Military Lodge of the Regiment of Foot*

- George Walton, *Solomon's Lodge, Georgia*

- William Whipple, *St. John's Lodge, New Jersey*

In addition to these signatories of the Declaration of Independence, 33 general officers of the Continental Army were Freemasons. Other notables included Benjamin Franklin, Ambassador to France during the American Revolution and Provincial Grand Master of Pennsylvania, and Paul Revere, who became Grand Master of Massachusetts. The cause of American freedom attracted Masonic supporters from other countries as well, among them two of General Washington's most valued officers: the Marquis de Lafayette from France and Friedrich Wilhelm von Steuben from Prussia. The "father of the American Navy," the Scottish-born Admiral John Paul Jones, was also Mason, as was, alas, the notorious traitor General Benedict Arnold. (Freemasonry tries to make good men better but does not always succeed!)

Some thought was given to organizing an overarching "Grand Lodge of the United States," with George Washington as the first Grand Master, but the idea was short-lived. The various state Grand Lodges did not want to diminish their own authority by agreeing to such a body, so the practice of each state forming its own Grand Lodge became the norm.

The First Masonic President

George Washington, the first president of the United States, was an active Freemason as the member of a lodge in Virginia. The principles of Brotherly Love, Relief, and Truth to which he had been exposed as part of the Freemasons' Craft were among the virtues to which he aspired personally and in his role as Father of his Nation. One of the central purposes of Masonic Initiation—to teach one to dream better dreams—was one of the keys to success throughout his career. Washington knew that people become great by how they are inspired to use their minds. Freemasonry, for its part, teaches that there is a hidden power at the center of the human mind that can be tapped only by an Initiate who is properly prepared. As a passionate Free-

mason who was initiated at a young age—he was only 21 when he became a Master Mason in the Fredericksburg Lodge—Washington acquired qualities that would be the hallmark of his leadership.

Washington's father, Augustine, died when George was eleven years old, at which time he and his mother, Mary Ball Washington, went to live at Mount Vernon. This plantation, located on the Potomac River in the colony of Virginia, was owned by George's half-brother Lawrence. At age 16, George got job as a surveyor working for Thomas, Lord Fairfax, formerly of Denton Hall in Yorkshire. Fairfax was the Freemason we met in Chapter 7 as a Grand Master of the Grand Lodge of York. He was also a major landowner in Virginia. For three years, George surveyed Fairfax's lands in the Shenandoah Valley, working alongside Fairfax's younger brother Robert. The Fairfaxes had all been active Freemasons in the Grand Lodge of York; George's elder brother Lawrence had been educated in England and was married to Lord Fairfax's niece. Young George Washington became interested in the Craft while he worked for Lord Fairfax.

In 1751, George and Lawrence Washington sailed to Barbados in hopes of finding a climate that would help Lawrence's poor health. The Fairfaxes also owned land in Barbados, and Lawrence stayed there with his wife's family while George returned to Mount Vernon. Lawrence's health was failing, however, and he went home to die on July 26, 1752. George inherited Mount Vernon.

Three months later, on Saturday, November 4, 1752, he joined Fredericksburg Lodge No. 4, and shortly thereafter was made a military adjutant by Governor Dinwiddie, a friend of Lord Fairfax. In that capacity, Washington carried messages between French and English forces fighting each other along the U.S.–Canadian border. On the first Saturday of March, 1753, he was granted leave from his military duties to be made a Fellowcraft Mason in Fredericksburg. On Saturday, August 4, 1753, he attended the lodge again to be made a Master Mason. The Fredericksburg lodge followed the Scottish Rite and, six years after his initiation, it was awarded a charter from the Scottish Grand Lodge to formalize its position.

Jump ahead to the American Revolution: In 1777, the Marquis de Lafayette, a French aristocrat, military officer, and Freemason, joined Washington's army and became his close friend. In 1784, Lafayette presented Bro. Washington with a Masonic apron embroidered by his wife. Lafayette chose the symbols on the apron to inspire Washington in the final military campaigns against the British and the transition to nationhood. Washington would always wear the apron with great pride.

Meanwhile, in December 1778, while serving as commander in chief of the Continental Army, General Washington celebrated the Masonic Feast of St. John the Evangelist and took part in a Masonic parade in White Plains, New York. The following June, he celebrated the other Feast of St. John—John the Baptist—at a Masonic Festival held by the American Union Military Lodge at West Point. Later in 1779, he was offered the position of Grand Master Mason of the United States, but declined it because of his military commitments. He did join Alexandria Lodge No. 39 in Virginia, however, and became its Worshipful Master.

After Americans captured the lodge chest and warrant of the Lodge of Social and Military Virtues—No. 227 on the roll of the Grand

Lodge of Ireland and attached to the 46th Foot Regiment of the British Army—the items were returned to the original regiment by an honor guard under a flag of truce on the orders of General Washington.

When Washington was sworn in as the first president of the United States on April 30, 1789, he took the oath of office on a Volume of The Sacred Law borrowed from St. John's Lodge No. 1 New York. Early in his second term, on September 18, 1793, he laid the cornerstone for the United States Capitol in Washington, D.C., acting as Masonic Presiding Master in a ceremony conducted in full Masonic regalia and working the full Masonic ritual for laying a cornerstone.

Meanwhile, the dollar was adopted as the unit of currency for the United States, symbolized by an "S" with a double vertical strike-

through (although it often appears in print today with a single vertical slash). The "S" was borrowed from the symbol for an old Spanish coin, but the two vertical lines represent the two Mason pillars—Boaz and Jachin—from the porch of King Solomon's Temple.

On December 27, 1792—the Winter Feast of St. John celebrated by Masons—President Washington completed 40 years of service to Freemasonry. To mark the occasion, the Freemasons of Boston presented him with an inscribed Book of Constitutions (which sets out the rules of running a Masonic Lodge). His letter of thanks read as follows:

> *Flattering as it may be to the human mind, and truly honourable as it is, to receive from our fellow-citizens testimonies of approbation for exertions to promote the public welfare; it is not less pleasing to know, that*

the milder virtues of the heart are highly respected by a Society whose liberal principles are founded in the immutable laws of truth and justice.

To enlarge the sphere of social happiness is worthy of the benevolent design of a Masonic Intuition; and it is most fervently to be wished, that the conduct of every member of the fraternity, as well as those publications that discover the principles which actuate them, may tend to convince mankind, that the grand object of Masonry is to promote the happiness of the human race.

While I beg your acceptance of my thanks for "the Book of Constitutions" which you have sent me, and for the honour you have done me in the Dedication, permit me to assure you, that I feel all those emotions of gratitude which your affectionate Address and cordial wishes are calculated to inspire; and I sincerely pray that the Great Architect of the Universe may bless you here, and receive you hereafter in his immortal temple."

When Washington was buried at Mount Vernon on December 18, 1799, his Lodge brethren paid him full Masonic funeral honors.

Not to be overlooked in this history is that fact that even such an upright Mason as George Washington kept slaves, who were barred from becoming Freemasons. The man who changed all that was an African America Mason who was initiated by an English lodge. His name was Prince Hall, and he benefited from the fact that there were Freemasons on both sides of the War of Independence and that they all sought to uphold the Masonic principles, of Brotherly Love, Relief, and Truth.

PRINCE HALL

The Prince Hall Masonic Lodges

The African Lodge of Massachusetts has the only original Charter issued by the Grand Lodge of England (the predecessor to today's United Grand Lodge of England) still existing in the United States. The Charter was awarded to the first master of a lodge of Black Americans, Worshipful Brother Prince Hall. He was born in 1735 either in Barbados or Africa—there is some dispute. What we do know for certain is that he arrived in Boston in 1765 as a slave. He was sold to a man named William Hall and called Prince. Hall was so impressed with him that he granted Prince his freedom in 1770. Taking the surname of his former master and friend, he became known as Prince Hall.

Although Prince Hall had not been allowed to become a Mason while he was a slave, he knew that his beliefs in freedom and equality coincided with those of the Craft. He began to speak at public meetings, calling for equal treatment for black people, education for black children and the abolition of slavery, but he became convinced that people did not listen to him because he was a black man. The Boston Tea Party convinced him that the people of the city listened to what Freemasons had to say and valued the same ideals. Because all

THE WASHINGTON MASONIC NATIONAL MEMORIAL
in Alexandria, Virginia

When he was sworn in as the first president of the United States in 1789, George Washington was the Master of Alexandria Lodge No. 39, on the roll of the Grand Lodge of Virginia. When he died ten years later, the Lodge was officially redesignated Alexandria-Washington Lodge No. 22.

Washington's family and friends donated many of Bro George's Masonic memorabilia to the lodge, but its rooms were not the best place to store and display these irreplaceable items. Many of the relics were destroyed by fire in 1871.

A member of Alexandria-Washington Lodge, Bro. Charles Callahan, was so concerned about preserving the remaining memorabilia that he bought a plot of land on Shooter's (or Shuter's) Hill in 1909 and donated it to the lodge as the site of a proposed new, fireproof building. The lodge was unable to afford a suitable facility, however, so the Grand Master of Virginia, Joseph Eggleston, called a meeting of all interested Masons on February 22, 1910—Washington's Birthday. The attendees established the George Washington Masonic National Memorial Association, and Bro. Thomas Shryock, the Grand Master Mason of Maryland, became its first president. The Memorial Association resolved that it would not borrow money for the project and that the construction would proceed only as sufficient funds were donated by American Masons. It took 60 years to raise the money to complete the work.

Bro. President Calvin Coolidge laid the Memorial's foundation stone on November 1, 1923. President Herbert Hoover officially opened the building and dedicated it to Washington's memory on May 12, 1932, the bicentennial year of Washington's birth. The massive granite structure was topped by a tower, modelled after the Lighthouse of Alexandria in ancient Egypt, that rose more than 300 feet in the air. The interior of the memorial—featuring Lodge meeting halls, elaborate architectural appointments, statues, murals, and a host of symbolic elements—was not finished until 1970.

According to the George Washington Masonic National Memorial Association, the mission of the organization and the monument is:

To inspire humanity through education to emulate and promote the virtues, character and vision of George Washington, the Man, the Mason and Father of our Country.

The museum, still privately funded by Masonic contributions, is open to the public seven days a week "to honor and perpetuate the memory, character and virtues of the man who best exemplifies what Freemasons are and ought to be, Brother George Washington."

the influential people in Boston seemed to be Freemasons, Hall concluded that he must join the Order if he wanted to get people to listen to his message.

Even as a free man and entitled to be considered, Hall was turned down several times in his efforts to join Boston Masonic Lodges. Finally in 1775, the Master of Lodge No. 441 of the Grand Lodge of Ireland, attached to the 38th British Foot Infantry in Boston, heard of his ambition and granted his petition for membership. On March 6, Hall and 14 other free men of color were regularly initiated at a meeting of Military Lodge No. 441 at Castle William Island. They were

the first black men to become Masons in America, and when the British left Boston in 1776, Prince Hall was given a permit from No. 441 to meet with his fellow initiates as a lodge. It was to be known as African Lodge No. 1, and Hall was its Worshipful Master.

Prince Hall successfully petitioned General Washington to allow black men to join the Army and then signed up himself. He fought at the Battle of Bunker Hill on June 17, 1775, where Joseph Warren, Grand Master of the Grand Lodge of Massachusetts, was killed by a British musket ball, and then served with distinction under General William Prescott. After the war, Hall set up as a leather-dresser and was so successful that he was able to buy his property. He became a registered voter by 1787 and persuaded the Massachusetts legislature to pass a bill to protect freed slaves from being kidnapped and sold back into slavery in the South. And while he also ran a school for Negro children at his own home in Boston, Hall is best remembered for his longtime interest in promoting and developing Freemasonry as a positive influence on black men.

Bro. Hall had a permit to work African Lodge No. 1, but he did not have a warrant for the lodge to initiate more Masons. He decided to do something about that. On March 2, 1784, he wrote to the Grand Lodge of England, explaining about his permit and petitioning for a warrant that would enable the lodge to initiate new Masons as well as just meet. In response, the Grand Lodge of England issued African Lodge No. 459, with a charter on September 29, 1784. It thus became the first regular lodge of black men in America.

The African Lodge grew to such an extent that Worshipful Master Prince Hall was appointed Provincial Grand Master in 1791, founding the first Black Provincial Grand Lodge. In that capacity, Hall in 1797 authorized a new lodge in Philadelphia and another one in

Rhode Island. The two new lodges were granted charters from African Lodge No. 459.

In December 1808, a year after Prince Hall's death, African Lodge No. 459 (Boston), African Lodge No. 459 (Philadelphia), and Hiram Lodge No. 3 (Providence) called a general assembly of the Craft and organized the African Grand Lodge, also known as African Grand Lodge No. I. In 1847, out of respect for their founding father, they changed the name to the Prince Hall Grand Lodge—as is it still called today. In 1848, Union Lodge No. 2, Rising Sons of St. John No.3, and Celestial Lodge No. 4 became the first lodges to be chartered by the Prince Hall Grand Lodge.

There are now some 5,000 lodges and 47 grand lodges that trace their lineage to the Prince Hall Grand Lodge Jurisdiction of Massachusetts. Racial segregation across North American in the 19th and early 20th centuries made it difficult for black Americans to join lodges outside the Prince Hall jurisdictions, as there was no formal inter-jurisdictional recognition between parallel Masonic authorities. Today, however, most U.S. Grand Lodges recognize their Prince Hall counterparts, which celebrate their heritage as lodges for black Americans but are open to all prospective members, regardless of race or religion.

Masonry on the Moon

The first man on the moon was a "Lewis," the term for the child of a Freemason who has not yet been initiated The second man on the moon was an active Freemason The Vice-President who played an instrumental role in committing the United States to reaching the moon was a Freemason. The administrator of the Apollo Moon Land-ing Program was a Freemason, and the manager of the Apollo Program Command and Service Modules was a Freemason. It may come as no surprise, therefore, that a Masonic flag travelled to the moon and back on the first historic landing mission in July 1969. What may surprise you to learn, however, is that authority to hold Masonic lodges on the moon has been formally assigned to the Grand Lodge of Texas.

While President John F. Kennedy is famous for issuing the chal-lenge on May 25, 1961—"This nation should commit itself, before this decade is out, to landing a man on the moon and returning him safely to the earth"—Vice President Lyndon B. Johnson played the key role in establishing headquarters for the NASA astronaut corps, its manned space program, and Project Apollo in Houston, Texas, at the space center that later took his name. Kennedy was not a Free-mason, but Johnson had been initiated on October 30, 1937, at John-son City Lodge No. 561, in Johnson City, Texas.

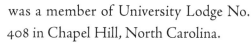

James Edwin Webb, the NASA Administrator from 1961 to 1968, was a member of University Lodge No. 408 in Chapel Hill, North Carolina.

Kenneth S. Kleinknecht, manager of the Apollo Program Command and Ser-vice Modules, was a member of Fairview Lodge No. 699 in Fairview, Ohio.

Neil A. Armstrong, Sr., the father of the commander of Apollo 11 and the first man on the moon, was a Grand Officer in the Grand Lodge of Ohio, making astronaut Neil a Lewis.

Edwin E. "Buzz" Aldrin, the co-pilot of Apollo 11 and second man on the moon, was a member of Clear Lake Lodge No. 1417, in Seabrook, Texas, at the time of the mission.

The heavy participation of Freemasons in the first moon landing was not the result, as some have suggested, of some Masonic conspiracy, but because many members are inspired by the traditional Craft incentive to study "the hidden mysteries of nature and science." Thus, when Freemasons in NASA were given the chance to fly to the moon, they drew on their Masonic values and tradition to make the most of the opportunity. As the website of the Grand Lodge of British Colombia and Yukon puts it:

> *Freemasons have always been in the forefront of the scientific community; from the founding of the British Royal Society to today's NASA programme in the United States.*

Much as physicists Leo Szilard and Albert Einstein convinced Bro. President Franklin Roosevelt in 1939 that the atom bomb was sitting in the Platonic realm waiting to be revealed, James Webb used similar arguments to persuade Vice President Johnson and the Kennedy administration that the means to reach the moon were within the reach of American technology. For seven years after President Kennedy's historic challenge in May 1961, Webb politicked, coaxed, cajoled,

and maneuvered in Washington on behalf of NASA and the dream of reaching the moon. In the end, he built a seamless web of political connections that generated the resources and support to achieve the goal of Project Apollo according to the schedule President Kennedy had announced.

In November 1969, *The New Age Magazine* (now the *Scottish Rite Journal*) published a special edition celebrating the success of Project Apollo and praising the Masons involved in its success. Writing in that issue, Bro. Kenneth Kleinknecht, the manager of Command and Service Modules for the Apollo program, a manager in the Gemini and Skylab projects, and a member of Fairview Lodge No. 699, said:

> *Note how many of the astronauts themselves are Brother Masons: Edwin E. Aldrin, Jr.; L. Gordon Cooper, Jr.; Donn F. Eisle; Walter M. Schirra; Thomas P. Stafford; Edgar D. Mitchell, and Paul J. Weitz. Before his tragic death in a flash fire at Cape Kennedy on January 27, 1967, Virgil I. "Gus" Grissom was a Mason, too. Astronaut Gordon Cooper, during his epochal Gemini V spaceflight in August of 1965, carried with him an official Thirty-third Degree Jewel and a Scottish Rite flag. Via the lunar plaque, the Masonic insignia and flag, and the Masonic astronauts themselves — Masonry already is in the space age. Can we doubt Freemasonry and its spiritual relevance to the modern era when even its material representatives have today made historic inroads into the infinite expanses of outer space?*

Masonic jurisdiction over the moon was established by Bro. Edwin Eugene (Buzz) Aldrin, Jr., who carried with him a dispensation from

the Grand Lodge of Texas as a Special Deputy of the Grand Master, authorizing him to claim Masonic Territorial Jurisdiction over the Moon for the Most Worshipful Grand Lodge of Texas of Ancient Free and Accepted Masons. Upon his return to earth, Special Deputy Grand Master Aldrin certified that he carried the dispensation to the moon and that the jurisdiction was established on July 20, 1969. The Masonic flag he took with him, embroidered with the emblem of the Scottish Rite, is now housed in the Museum of the Supreme Council Scottish Rite in Washington, D.C.

On the basis of that dispensation, the Grand Lodge of Texas has warranted a lodge that is authorized to hold Masonic meetings and teach the philosophy and symbology of Freemasonry on the moon. Its name is Tranquillity Lodge 2000, and it holds meetings four times a year at various cities in Texas until such time as it can convened on the moon. The lodge's apron of the lodge depicts the earth as seen from the moon.

THE STUDY OF symbols has come a long way from the early stone-masons of Aberdeen, to the freedom fighters of the Boston Tea Party, the defenders of equality of Prince Hall, and the rocket scientists and astronauts of NASA. And yet, through the centuries, the teachings of Freemasonry and the meaning of its symbols remain essentially the same. The rocket scientists, the Prince Hall Brethren, the founders of American democracy, and the stoneworkers of medieval Aberdeen all have shared their work in the most basic sense.

Each knows that Freemasonry is a peculiar system of morality veiled in allegory and illustrated by symbols.

FURTHER READING

Butler, Alan, and John Richie. *Rosslyn Revealed: A Library in Stone.* John Hunt Publishing: Ropley, UK, 2006.

Hay, Gilbert. *The Prose Works of Sir Gilbert Hay*, Vol. II. Edinburgh: Scottish Text Society, 1993.

Lomas, Robert. *Freemasonry and the Birth of Modern Science.* Rockport, MA: Fair Winds Press, 2003.

Lomas, Robert. *Turning The Hiram Key.* Rockport, MA: Fair Winds Press, 2005.

Lomas, Robert. *Turning The Solomon Key.* Rockport, MA: Fair Winds Press, 2006.

Lomas, Robert. *The Secrets of Freemasonry*, London: Constable and Robinson, 2006.

Lomas, Robert. *Turning The Templar Key.* Rockport, MA: Fair Winds Press, 2009.

Lomas, Robert. *The Secret Science of Masonic Initiation.* Weiser Books: San Francisco, 2010.

Lomas, Robert. *The Lost Key.* London: Hodder and Stoughton, 2010.

Lomas, Robert. *The Secret Power of Masonic Symbols.* Rockport, MA: Fair Winds Press, 2011.

Lomas, Robert. *The Lewis Guide to Masonic Symbols.* London: Lewis Masonic, 2013.

MacNulty, W. Kirk. *Freemasonry: Symbols, Secrets, Significance.* London: Thames & Hudson, 2006

MacNulty, W. Kirk. *Freemasonry: A Journey Through Ritual and Symbol.* London: Thames & Hudson, 1991

Stevenson, David. *The Origins of Freemasonry.* New York: Cambridge University Press, 1988.

Wilmhurst, Walter Leslie. *The Meaning of Masonry.* Reprint of 1923 edition. New York: Bell Publishing, 1980.

Archives and Websites

Aberdeen Burgh Records (1483), vol. I, no 39. University of Dundee Digitized Archives.

Aberdeen Burgh Records (1493), vol. I, no. 52. University of Dundee Digitized Archives.

Scottish Rite of Freemasonry, Supreme Council 330, Southern Jurisdiction, U.S.A.: *http://scottishrite.org*

George Washington Masonic National Memorial: *www.gwmemorial.org*

Grand Lodge of Scotland: *www.grandlodgescotland.com*

Grand Lodge of Texas: *www.grandlodgeoftexas.org* (and see Grand Lodges of other states)

United Grand Lodge of England: *www.ugle.org.uk*

University of Bradford Online Masonic Archive: *www.brad.ac.uk/webofhiram*

About the Author

ROBERT LOMAS was initiated as a Freemason in 1986 and became a popular lecturer and author on Masonic history, ritual, and spirituality. His many books on the subject include the international bestseller *The Hiram Key* (1986, with Christopher Knight), as well as *Freemasonry and the Birth of Modern Science* (2003), *The Secret Science of Masonic Initiation* (2010), *The Secret Power of Masonic Symbols* (2011), and a host of others. He has also written on the Neolithic period, ancient engineering, archaeoastrononomy, and the inventor Nikola Tesla. Lomas has a B.Sc. in Electrical Engineering and a Ph.D. in solid-state physics, both from the University of Salford in England. He currently lectures on Information Systems at the University of Bradford's School of Management.

About the Illustrator

SARAH BECAN is a comics artist, author, and designer based in Chicago, and the illustrator of such books as *Astronomy For Beginners* (2008) and *The Adventures of Fat Rice* (2016). Becan's work has appeared in a variety of print and online publications, including *Saveur, Rodale's Organic Life, Eater.com, TruthOut.com,* and the collaborative serial collection *Cartozia Tales;* she is also the creator of the autobiographical webcomic "I Think You're Sauceome." Becan was awarded a Xeric Award and a Stumptown Trophy for Outstanding Debut in 2010 for her first graphic novel, *The Complete Ouija Interviews,* and her work has been nominated twice for the Ignatz Award. Her second graphic novel, *Shuteye,* was released in 2012.

THE FOR BEGINNERS® SERIES

ABSTRACT EXPRESSIONISM	ISBN 978-1- 939994-62-2
AFRICAN HISTORY FOR BEGINNERS	ISBN 978-1-934389-18-8
ANARCHISM FOR BEGINNERS	ISBN 978-1-934389-32-4
ARABS & ISRAEL FOR BEGINNERS	ISBN 978-1-934389-16-4
ART THEORY FOR BEGINNERS	ISBN 978-1-934389-47-8
ASTRONOMY FOR BEGINNERS	ISBN 978-1-934389-25-6
AYN RAND FOR BEGINNERS	ISBN 978-1-934389-37-9
BARACK OBAMA FOR BEGINNERS, AN ESSENTIAL GUIDE	ISBN 978-1-934389-44-7
BEN FRANKLIN FOR BEGINNERS	ISBN 978-1-934389-48-5
BLACK HISTORY FOR BEGINNERS	ISBN 978-1-934389-19-5
THE BLACK HOLOCAUST FOR BEGINNERS	ISBN 978-1-934389-03-4
BLACK PANTHERS FOR BEGINNERS	ISBN 978-1-939994-39-4
BLACK WOMEN FOR BEGINNERS	ISBN 978-1-934389-20-1
BUDDHA FOR BEGINNERS	ISBN 978-1-939994-33-2
BUKOWSKI FOR BEGINNERS	ISBN 978-1-939994-37-0
CHICANO MOVEMENT FOR BEGINNERS	ISBN 978-1-939994-64-6
CHOMSKY FOR BEGINNERS	ISBN 978-1-934389-17-1
CIVIL RIGHTS FOR BEGINNERS	ISBN 978-1-934389-89-8
CLIMATE CHANGE FOR BEGINNERS	ISBN 978-1-939994-43-1
DADA & SURREALISM FOR BEGINNERS	ISBN 978-1-934389-00-3
DANTE FOR BEGINNERS	ISBN 978-1-934389-67-6
DECONSTRUCTION FOR BEGINNERS	ISBN 978-1-934389-26-3
DEMOCRACY FOR BEGINNERS	ISBN 978-1-934389-36-2
DERRIDA FOR BEGINNERS	ISBN 978-1-934389-11-9
EASTERN PHILOSOPHY FOR BEGINNERS	ISBN 978-1-934389-07-2
EXISTENTIALISM FOR BEGINNERS	ISBN 978-1-934389-21-8
FANON FOR BEGINNERS	ISBN 978-1-934389-87-4
FDR AND THE NEW DEAL FOR BEGINNERS	ISBN 978-1-934389-50-8
FOUCAULT FOR BEGINNERS	ISBN 978-1-934389-12-6
FRENCH REVOLUTIONS FOR BEGINNERS	ISBN 978-1-934389-91-1
GENDER & SEXUALITY FOR BEGINNERS	ISBN 978-1-934389-69-0
GREEK MYTHOLOGY FOR BEGINNERS	ISBN 978-1-934389-83-6
HEIDEGGER FOR BEGINNERS	ISBN 978-1-934389-13-3
THE HISTORY OF CLASSICAL MUSIC FOR BEGINNERS	ISBN 978-1-939994-26-4
THE HISTORY OF OPERA FOR BEGINNERS	ISBN 978-1-934389-79-9
ISLAM FOR BEGINNERS	ISBN 978-1-934389-01-0
JANE AUSTEN FOR BEGINNERS	ISBN 978-1-934389-61-4
JUNG FOR BEGINNERS	ISBN 978-1-934389-76-8
KIERKEGAARD FOR BEGINNERS	ISBN 978-1-934389-14-0
LACAN FOR BEGINNERS	ISBN 978-1-934389-39-3
LIBERTARIANISM FOR BEGINNERS	ISBN 978-1-939994-66-0
LINCOLN FOR BEGINNERS	ISBN 978-1-934389-85-0
LINGUISTICS FOR BEGINNERS	ISBN 978-1-934389-28-7
MALCOLM X FOR BEGINNERS	ISBN 978-1-934389-04-1
MARX'S DAS KAPITAL FOR BEGINNERS	ISBN 978-1-934389-59-1
MCLUHAN FOR BEGINNERS	ISBN 978-1-934389-75-1
MORMONISM FOR BEGINNERS	ISBN 978-1-939994-52-3
MUSIC THEORY FOR BEGINNERS	ISBN 978-1-939994-46-2
NIETZSCHE FOR BEGINNERS	ISBN 978-1-934389-05-8
PAUL ROBESON FOR BEGINNERS	ISBN 978-1-934389-81-2
PHILOSOPHY FOR BEGINNERS	ISBN 978-1-934389-02-7
PLATO FOR BEGINNERS	ISBN 978-1-934389-08-9
POETRY FOR BEGINNERS	ISBN 978-1-934389-46-1
POSTMODERNISM FOR BEGINNERS	ISBN 978-1-934389-09-6
PROUST FOR BEGINNERS	ISBN 978-1-939994-44-8
RELATIVITY & QUANTUM PHYSICS FOR BEGINNERS	ISBN 978-1-934389-42-3
SARTRE FOR BEGINNERS	ISBN 978-1-934389-15-7
SAUSSURE FOR BEGINNERS	ISBN 978-1-939994-41-7
SHAKESPEARE FOR BEGINNERS	ISBN 978-1-934389-29-4
STANISLAVSKI FOR BEGINNERS	ISBN 978-1-939994-35-6
STRUCTURALISM & POSTSTRUCTURALISM FOR BEGINNERS	ISBN 978-1-934389-10-2
TESLA FOR BEGINNERS	ISBN 978-1-939994-48-6
TONI MORRISON FOR BEGINNERS	ISBN 978-1-939994-54-7
WOMEN'S HISTORY FOR BEGINNERS	ISBN 978-1-934389-60-7
UNIONS FOR BEGINNERS	ISBN 978-1-934389-77-5
U.S. CONSTITUTION FOR BEGINNERS	ISBN 978-1-934389-62-1
ZEN FOR BEGINNERS	ISBN 978-1-934389-06-5
ZINN FOR BEGINNERS	ISBN 978-1-934389-40-9